# Words of Wisdom
## Book 1

*The spiritual teachings of
Swami Premananda*

**For information about
Swami Premananda
www.sripremananda.org**

A comprehensive website in many languages about
Swami Premananda, his life and teachings, Sri Premananda Ashram,
Sri Premananda Centres and Youth Groups worldwide.

**Words of Wisdom Book 1**

**First edition
Copyright © 2016 Rishi Publications**

ISBN: 978-81-936202-5-0

Published by Rishi Publications, India

# Contents

# Introduction

Swami Premananda was an enlightened spiritual master. He was one of those rare great souls whose very presence brought about a state of peace and stillness. Often playful and full of humour he could also be both direct and subtle.

Swamiji radiated love and compassion which he practically shared in the form of constant selfless service. He always demonstrated a keen understanding of everyone, everything and every situation. His eyes reached deep into our very souls, seeing all and knowing all. His guidance is given in order to put us on a practical spiritual path and helps us to shift our focus to being aware of the higher consciousness within us.

Although Swamiji tells us that words cannot express the great joy and love that arises once we are established in that state of being, his individual way of expression allows us to glimpse its essence, its taste and its fragrance. When we read his words, we can also enjoy his vast energy, his love and laughter. They open up the way to our own peace of mind and happiness.

Swamiji left his physical body in February 2011, yet his teachings and extraordinary vibration live on.

# Foreword

**THE PERFECT SAGE**

*By Michel Coquet*

*Michel Coquet is a renowned scholar of Hinduism, esoteric Buddhism and Eastern philosophy. He is an accomplished practitioner and teacher of martial arts, the author of many books on martial arts and with his wife, Gisèle, on esoteric philosophy.*

In 1990 I was requested to accompany a group of 23 French spiritual seekers to India. For this tour I had to decide which of the serious ashrams and still-living authentic spiritual masters to visit. Around one year before that, I had heard about Swami Premananda. I was in a great hurry to meet this master, about whom people spoke with much admiration. Unfortunately, our programme was very full, and we could only allocate three days to visit Swamiji and, as I was responsible for the group, I was afraid that such a meeting might not fit in with the wishes of the other tour members. Not only that, during a meeting with a realized being anything and everything was possible, the experience might not be transcendent and might simply consist of a test with the aim of finding out those who were merely curious and those who were genuinely interested in spirituality. A sage often needs a certain period of time in order to determine what motivates the pilgrims on their spiritual path. Therefore, I had some apprehensions, not being aware of the omniscience of Swamiji and his capacity to know immediately the quality of a seeker, as well as the nature of one's past experiences. Indeed, the meeting was going to be an exceptional experience for the group – as well as for the author.

Saturday and Sunday were the privileged days when the devotees got the opportunity of meeting Swamiji individually. During this meeting, Swamiji was in a state of meditation and everyone could submit their problems to him and receive his blessings. My mind was solely occupied with the group, and the first thing Swamiji said to me was not to worry and that he would take care of the group and make them all happy! I have to admit that he fulfilled his promise far beyond my hopes that very evening.

Many members of the group wanted to ask Swamiji questions concerning his extraordinary powers which he manifested on special religious occasions. The fact that he could materialize kilos of vibhūti (holy ash) and lingams through his mouth or make whatever he willed appear through a movement of his hand, naturally aroused enquiry and some doubts.

On the last evening, Swamiji kindly allowed me to perform a pāda pūjā (ritual washing and anointing of Swamiji's feet), which I personally feel is a religious act during which the ego is surrendered to the Guru. I will keep this pāda pūjā in my heart as one of the most wonderful ceremonies I have ever experienced.

After this, Swamiji invited us to ask any questions we wished. Swamiji continued late into the night and, seeing that our eyelids were becoming heavy, he generously agreed to continue the satsang the following morning.

That last day, just after the morning pūjā, the satsang continued. Swami was wearing a simple traditional cloth wrapped around his waist called a dhoti, and the upper part of his body was not covered. He came and sat with us like a father in the midst of his children. As the main questions had been asked, I dared to ask a last question concerning the benefit of the practice of japa, the chanting of mantras. After explaining to us about the method and effect of this practice, Swamiji rubbed his empty hands together and from his right hand a japamālā made of small rudrāksha seeds appeared, which he threw in my direction. Our group only had eyes for him and Swamiji, guessing the desire of some others to get a mālā as well, materialized some more japamālās in the same manner. Then he said he would give them small Shivalingams in metal which he also materialized. One of us preferred to have a Ganesh statue, and Swamiji materialized one, again simply with a movement of his hand. It was a morning which we will never forget.

We were all ready to leave when Swamiji displayed

extreme kindness by taking us to a large and famous
temple in Trichy which is consecrated to Mariamma, an
aspect of the Divine Mother who is also the Goddess of
rain. Sri Premananda Ashram pays particular attention
to the female principle, and the women in Swamiji's
āshram are allowed to perform pūjā as Brahmin priests
do in the temples. I have never seen this in India before,
even though some great teachers, perceiving the coming
of a cycle which will establish again the once-dominant
female principle complementary to the male principle,
have left their ashrams in the charge of a woman after
their own passing.

Entry to the temple is often not allowed to non-Hindus,
but the presence of the master lifted all restrictions,
and the group could enter the heart of the sanctuary
to worship. Afterwards, we sat together in one of the
temple halls and Swami Premananda explained to us the
significance of the temple and its various symbols.

After we had taken lunch in a restaurant, Swamiji
came to say goodbye and returned to the Ashram. The
group realized that they had enjoyed the privilege of
exceptional grace.

My mind was so strongly impressed with the whole
experience that I decided to return with my wife, Gisèle,
for Mahāshivarātri in 1991. However, the Gulf War
postponed this plan, and we had to wait until June. The
few months between the two journeys allowed me to
deepen the spiritual relationship with the master and,
during the second visit, we were able to experience the
love of Swami Premananda more deeply.

One can only love and admire such a master, who, with
an incomparable skill, handled the power of the word and

the knowledge of the heart. Swami Premananda was pure energy, always in action, giving instructions unceasingly to construct buildings and to plant trees, teaching and guiding the orphans who were given a home there, all the while overseeing his āshram. His actions had the authenticity of the perfect sage and were never predictable.

His only wish is to lead us to the feet of the Lord, to the realization of the Self, and in order to do this with sensitivity and intuition, he dissolves or breaks our mental structures, our artificial supports, our concepts and prejudices. He disorganizes our concrete and rational mind and stimulates us to question ourselves unceasingly by subtly provoking circumstances in a manner that obliges the student to adapt, at any instant, to new and unforeseeable structures. All this is in order that habit should never be allowed to take over in the present moment and that one is always in constant awareness.

Putting our patience through a hard test, Swamiji makes us conscious of time being an illusion which can easily be dissolved by going inside and concentrating on the inner presence of the Self, which transcends time and space. Through his behaviour towards us he pushes us towards the present moment, not giving time to regret or to remember a past gone forever. In the same way, he does not let us look forward to goals of a hypothetical future.

Our equanimity is also tested, but it is his capacity to stir up our love, not only towards his form but also towards his divine teachings, which very much include how to know our own Self, which predominantly persuade us of his greatness as a teacher. In this way, he prevents the danger of attachment to or dependence on his exterior form, which, as we know, is always the main problem in the relationship between a teacher and disciple.

As we have understood it, the essential message of Swamiji is simple – to inform the world that a spiritual power exists which is omnipresent and which we call God. It is unique and worshipped in different forms in each religion. This unique God lives in the heart of all existence and has to be realized by every human being. To realize that we are one and that we are a particle of Divinity can only be accomplished by changing our ways of thinking and living. The mind is the key to our imprisonment as well as to our liberation. Peace and freedom from the limitations of thought can be attained through meditation. Before this, the mind has to be calmed and purified through ritual and right attitude in the heart while in the midst of day-to-day life.

The right attitude consists of the eradication of the belief that one is the body, in perceiving unity in diversity, in detaching oneself from the fruit of action, in loving without object – because the nature of the soul is love – in controlling one's passions and in having only one desire, the desire to be united with God.

He showed us that spiritual discipline must allow us to transform a competitive mind into a cooperative mind, to change desire into love, and, even more progressively, to abandon our attraction towards the experiencing of what is outside in order to replace it by the knowledge of the Self.

I did not immediately understand the technique taught by Swamiji. Today it seems to me that he did not have a specific technique but that he worked individually on each aspirant according to their capacities and deep tendencies. He was beyond methods and gave complete freedom to his students, yet he corrected and rectified the discipline that was undertaken by each individual. Even though he recognized the validity of the ritual and of pūjās as means of purification, he truly seemed to act in the spirit of non-duality. Swamiji knew the art of inducing reactions and through that he brought to light the presence of the covered ego. I experienced this myself, and I consider that the short time I stayed in his presence has indeed brought forth and allowed me to rectify certain of my own limitations. It seems to me that Swamiji merged the ideas and practices of the great saints Sri Ramanujacharya and Sri Shankaracharya with a background of pure devotion, for without devotion even the best discipline would remain sterile.

We had intended to visit the sacred mountain of Arunachala in Tiruvannamalai, Tamil Nadu, before the end of our stay, with a view to writing a book about this marvellous place. Swamiji asked us to come back to the Ashram before returning to France. On the evening of our departure, he invited us to his interview room in the Pūjā Hall. Here he asked us to close our hands because he was going to materialize statues. My wife chose the Divine Mother and, even though I was most attracted to the form of the Shivalingam, I did not make a real choice. Swamiji concentrated and, still smiling, invited us to open our hands. To our great joy and surprise in my wife's hands was the Goddess she had chosen and in mine, there had appeared a Ganesha made of five metals. Swamiji explained about the special powers in each statue. I never doubted divine manifestations coming forth from the body of Swami Premananda in the form of lingams or vibhūti, but if I had any doubts, this experience would have been enough to remove them.

I am not in a position to convey the very essence of my āshram experience because, as Dakshinamurti[1], Swami Premananda teaches through silence. It is a true communion from soul to soul, a spiritual transmission of his force and love which slowly eradicates our egoistic tendencies and awakens in us a reality which is both inclusive and transcendent towards the God from whom we are made. There is no word which can translate what such a Guru represents. We could only observe his actions with attention and vigilance and understand his messages, realizing that even the smallest of his words were always charged with deep significance – which we must discover for ourselves during meditation. To talk about the master while you live with him is almost impossible. What is there to say if one has just spent a few days in his ashram? There is one thing for sure – we can judge the tree by its fruits. We would not dare to judge the master, but we could see the quality of his discipline and feel the atmosphere of the Ashram. There we found a purity, a simplicity, a non-sectarian and non-dogmatic spirit and, in the reception we received, we found much generosity, love and sincerity.

One cannot forget such experiences which bring hope for a better world in which masters like Swamiji endeavour to serve with greatness, strength and compassion. After having received so much, it was our wish to participate as much as we could in the ever-increasing global, spiritual renewal, supported by the blessings of Swami Premananda.

Jai Prema Shanti!

---

[1] A form of the deity Shiva who silently transmits spiritual wisdom

# Notes on the translation

Most of these talks and writings by Swami Premananda were in the Tamil language, and some were in English. Swamiji's mother tongue was Tamil.

In Tamil, there are different words for God with varied meanings, which we have translated as God or the Divine. It is important to note that Swamiji very often used the Tamil word *kadavul*, which means the One who is both immanent and transcendent, both within and beyond. At other times Swamiji spoke of the Supreme, the Absolute, the One without name or form, or the Universal Force and these instances have been recorded in the text.

# Be open-minded

There are many concepts to remember in spiritual life. These are very simple ideas but, at first, they might be difficult to follow.

It is better not to be narrow-minded and have fixed ideas about a person or a subject. You become narrow-minded because you are always judging – judging a situation, judging a person, thinking, "He is a bad man" or "She is a bad person." The next day you will find that you did not know all the facts and he is a good man, but others had told lies about him or that she is, in fact, a very nice person who was the victim of gossip. The mind is always changing, and what we see on the surface is often not the reality, the truth. You can never know the full truth of any matter until you have reached a certain mature stage of spiritual development. So it is better not to judge too much but to wait patiently and see what unfolds.

One can certainly never, ever judge the spiritual level of any other person. Some people might practise meditation from morning to night and never attain anything because their minds are not pure and are running from one subject to another. A simple person, carrying out their daily duty or service to humanity with pure devotion, inwardly offering every action to God, might suddenly become enlightened. So who are you to judge what spiritual maturity is? Rather than looking at the progression of others, use that mental energy to look at yourself. It is only the grace of God or your sadguru that can help you progress quickly. It's better to repeat God's name sincerely and always think of your spiritual master and his or her ideals rather than thinking about what others are doing.

Jealousy is a huge problem. Although many people generally tend to be jealous, it is more prevalent amongst ladies. This was, and still is, a problem for many spiritual masters. Generally speaking, ladies do not like it if other ladies develop quickly in spirituality. This is because they have a deep-rooted insecurity. They do not like it if the spiritual master gives attention to someone else. I feel that ladies should come up in spirituality. I want them to develop, mature and be accepted as great spiritual people. I like to teach them and show the world how great they are, but it is a very difficult task. They need to have more self-confidence and less attachment.

Learn to respect everybody. *Everybody*. If you do not speak and act with respect for everyone, then you have a long way to go on the spiritual path. God is within everyone and everything. If you really believe that and keep it in mind, then you cannot go wrong. But the trouble is, in an instant you forget it. Another way to cultivate a respectful mind is to think that everyone you meet has been sent by your spiritual master. Respect others in the same way you would respect your master. Take your spiritual teacher as an example of patience and respect. He does not get angry with the devotees. He has the patience to listen to and help everyone. Try to be like that. You must learn humility. This is so important. Do not think that you have grown up spiritually. This is purely ego.

Try not to aspire to lead a spiritual life thinking that you will gain position or become a sannyāsin or a teacher of others. Think that you know nothing and be as a little child. If you go to a spiritual place or a Sri Premananda Centre or visit our Ashram in India, think that the divine energy there should enter you and that you must get the maximum amount of blessings. This is the correct attitude. If you think you should get powers, or money, or control over others, or name and fame, I feel it is better that you stay in your own country and work hard. You can earn a lot of money and have a really worldly life.

You see, you must be very, very pure hearted to attain a high spiritual state; otherwise, ego will somehow creep into your mind and spoil all your progress. That is why I take you very slowly but surely on the path. First, we must clean all the egoism out of you and then only can we pour divine grace into you!

# Adaptability

Why waste your time thinking about the mental state of others? Sometimes you feel that others behave in a mad way. Remember, everyone, including you, has their own kind of madness. Each one is a little mad. This is a mad world, is it not? If you feel that a person or a situation is very difficult to deal with, try to be patient and learn from that situation or person. With self-control, calmness and love you can adjust to any situation in life. Such adaptability is very necessary in spirituality. You may find more complex situations in a spiritual centre or organization like our Ashram or the Sri Premananda Centres because everyone is undergoing purifications of some kind. That is because they are in contact with the divine energy more intensely. In the world, you can easily avoid many problems but by dealing carefully with devotees you experience and learn.

You can observe the faults of others but not judge them. Rather, try to understand them and then you can learn to fathom out your own faults. It is good to take the attitude that you will be tolerant of other people's bad qualities. At the same time, you must be perfect! I want you all to be perfect. I can guide you towards perfection, but it helps if you listen to my advice and, more importantly, follow it.

You need to adapt yourself to any situation. If any sudden difficulty comes to you, quickly call on your spiritual master or ishtam (the form of Divinity you like best). Now see my situation. Suddenly I was arrested on false charges and thrown into jail. I did not waste my time crying, worrying and thinking too much. I immediately asked the jailers to bring my pūjā box as soon as possible. Premananda is always thinking of the Divine in any circumstances. I am not interested in anything else. Whatever I discuss, my mind is always with the Divine. Whatever I do, my mind is immersed in God. That is why whatever I say or do is divine, because I am always thinking of God.

I am very happy in the jail. I am very happy out of the jail. I make the very best of my life here in the jail. Here I do just the same as I do outside. I do pūjās, I meditate, and I teach spirituality.

Here the poor people who have had great misfortune in life, or who have made terrible mistakes, have a chance to really talk to me about their sufferings or the wrong things they did. They can really think about how to change themselves. Through me, God's grace comes to them. That is really worthwhile, isn't it? Whatever they tell me, I am not shocked or upset. My heart is pure. I am here to help everyone. I think of everyone as my own child. I am mother and father to even the most hardened criminal.

God has given this work to me, so I do it whole-heartedly, wherever God sends me. God has chosen to send me to jail to do divine work and I accept this mission gladly. Likewise, I hope that you will all learn to accept any situations and problems.

Listen to the sublime consciousness within you. Do God's work without worrying about personal results and expectations. Try to be free from personal preferences, free from wanting power or self-satisfaction, free from jealousy, desire... all these things must slowly disappear, and you will see only the will of the Divine. When you see only the Divine, then you will always be happy. Wherever you are, whatever you have to do, wherever the Divine may send you, you will always be happy.

# Modern culture
# and traditional life

There are many different cultures in the world, but it is the present-day lifestyle that is really spoiling peoples' minds. Why? Because it is becoming more and more unnatural. It is so far removed from nature. Also, the mind is becoming more and more involved with this unnatural, modern culture and all its products. The mind has so many more material and worldly matters to become involved with that it gets further and further removed from spirituality. In times gone by people involved their minds more in spirituality because they did not have all these diverse kinds of material things, enjoyments and a false environment of superficial pleasures.

Now, in the modern world, your mind will want to drive a car. Preferably a fast, streamlined car with all kinds of gadgets. At the same time, it will want to listen to the sound system in the car. So the mind is totally lost in the car.

You always want to pamper your body. It wants perfect buildings to live in. It wants tiled showers, beautiful toilets, lovely cosmetics and shampoos to use. Then it likes many channels on the TV, it likes different kinds of drinks and drugs to forget problems with, it wants beautiful women or handsome men…it wants an endless stream of fashionable clothes, make-up and perfumes in order to attract the opposite sex. Isn't it all so false, empty and temporary…and finally tiring without any peace of mind? Desires are endless. You can never stop wanting and pampering and buying and saving for the next thing and looking forward to buying or doing something in the material world.

Today's young generation is totally involved in illusion. The television caters totally to this illusion and they would like to watch it for 24 hours a day. So, I have briefly described the modern world's illusory tendencies. Now I will tell you about the natural environment that is conducive to leading a spiritual life.

What is a traditional life? Firstly, even the house you live in would be made of simple, natural products. It should be plain with the minimum of furniture, clean and set in a natural place. A spiritual environment essentially should be clean and simple. There should not be too many things around you that fill up the mind with unnecessary thoughts and ideas. For a successful spiritual life, you need have with you only what is necessary. That is why traditional monks and nuns live in a cell (rather like a prison cell) with the minimum of facilities. They are expected to keep their rooms very clean.

There is a Tamil saying, 'cleanliness brings well-being.' In English, you say that 'cleanliness is next to godliness.' And this is really true. Divine energy likes a clean heart. In order to train for that, you first need to clean up your outer environment. However, if you become totally enlightened like the great beggar saint, Yogi Ramsuratkumar, who lived in Tiruvannamalai in Tamil Nadu, you can live in the dirtiest of places and it will not matter. But you are far from that yet. So keep yourself and your place really spotless. It is a great mental discipline. Don't keep lots of excess furniture, books, gadgets, clothes and so on. Have a good clear-out. It will really help you on your spiritual path. Everything has its own vibration. Clear out the old and unwanted. Clear up outside and then clean up inside.

Reduce your wants and desires to what is absolutely necessary. Eat a simple but pure diet. Under no circumstances should you take hallucinatory drugs. Try to reduce alcohol and then cut it out. Stop smoking. It spoils your mental and physical health and also that of others.

I am not asking you to be celibate (unless you live in the Ashram for some time – there it is a rule), but I do encourage you to have only one partner. You are all the more blessed if your partner is also interested in spirituality. Make the best of your love and togetherness. Support each other and help each other on the path, like two oars on a boat pulling towards the shores of spirituality.

Try to reduce your TV watching. Instead, do something spiritual; have more satsangs, sing bhajans, meditate or arrange more pūjās.

# Divine love

All subjects in the world have a master: classes in school, art, science, meditation – all are taught by some master. What subject has no master? LOVE!! Love is without a master. I am speaking of divine, pure love. The divine love (prema) that gives absolute, ultimate freedom and real happiness (ānandam).

Divine love is always there. It is the greatest force in the universe, and it is there inside each and every one of you. Only most of you don't feel it. What a pity, because it is available 24 hours a day and it is free to everyone.

Many people have closed up their hearts. They have closed the doors of their precious hearts and thrown away the key. So I have come to you firstly to find that key, to help you remember where you threw it and make you forget why you threw it away. Then I will help you open up your heart. When we have opened the doors, I will show you how to clean up your heart. You see, the doors have been locked for a long time and inside it is full of dust and cobwebs. After cleaning it, I will show you how to enjoy the lovely bliss in your heart. Finally, I will explain to you how to give that pure and wonderful love to others so that they too can open up their poor hearts.

Why have you closed up your hearts? You are too busy with so many other things to ever take the time to go into your heart and enjoy the bliss that is your true nature. You are full of yourself, full of ego and so concerned with your body and its endless desires. You don't make time or give priority to anything else. There is no room for the divine part of you and no time to look inside, deep into your lovely heart. How can you neglect your heart so much?

I know about your real heart. The true heart of a human being is full of spirituality. It is only your heart that can really make you happy, but you wander off to explore all the other parts of your body and make full use of them before, finally, as a last resort, you look into your heart. Then only you say, "Ah, why didn't I look in here first?" And so I have decided to come and explain to you all about your true heart in order that you don't have to waste years and years exploring everything else.

As you think, so you become. For every action, there is a reaction. I am always telling you these things. If you really want to know, understand and experience true, pure love you need to go into your real heart, discover the Divine and love the Divine. The more you think of the Divine and unblock yourself, the more you will become divine yourself. You see, it is very simple. I always think of the Divine. I always identify myself with the Divine.

Unfortunately, the love between humans is normally illusory. It is not true love. Try to see the Divine in your loved one. This will help you. Your love for your partner or child or relatives and friends will take on a purer and higher energy. Individual love is māyā, an illusion. Strive together towards the true love that is God.

Simply, how can you know real love? Show genuine love to everybody. Don't see their faults. See only their goodness and love that. You really do not need a master to instruct you how to love.

Open up and love the Divine! See it everywhere! Then surely its great energy will come into your heart more and more.

# True satsang

In order to have good and great spiritual satsang, first of all, everyone in the group needs to have some interest in spirituality. It does not matter if there are only a few of you in the group. Divine realization and service should be the only aim of everything you discuss and do.

If you put a rotten onion with good onions they will get spoiled. One person who has ulterior motives, such as collecting money or searching for a marriage partner on a worldly level, will spoil the spiritual aspirations of the others. It is good to be vigilant and protect your little satsang group. At the same time, try and help others – they may need it.

The power of the word is very great. Divinely inspired discussions do not need to be at a high intellectual level.

Very often, telling each other about simple spiritual experiences or relating incidents concerning the guru can bring a warm spiritual glow to the heart and mind. That pleasurable feeling will come from within, and the satsang will flow, naturally and spontaneously. You may start by reading the words of the guru, and then someone will remember an incident and relate it. Then another will add some comment. You can all learn and benefit from natural satsang.

Likewise, an ordinary conversation during which you say bad things about others can have a great negative influence. I am talking about gossip. Almost everyone gossips at some time or another. You may not think about it but gossip is like a drug. It is addictive and it pulls your consciousness down. It influences others to have bad feelings about your fellows, and it brings bad karma to the gossiper and the listener. Try to keep your consciousness at a high level and don't allow your mind to go down. Follow my advice – try not to gossip about others.

Try not to talk unnecessarily. For some time during the day be a little silent. At silent times you can go very deep inside. A small meditation daily is very helpful. During satsang with others, a group meditation in silence can be one of the most uplifting experiences. I don't mind if you get addicted to group meditation. That is infinitely more useful than hours and hours of useless talking. Group meditation is silent satsang. After your satsang discussions, communicate in a group with God. That is true satsang. I will definitely attend all your satsangs that are conducted sincerely and with a good goal. All such satsangs have my 'seal of approval' and my best blessings are with you. If you keep a chair or cushion for me, I will come and sit on it for sure. And I will show you that I came by some sign or another.

It does not matter if you are from the East or West, North or South. It does not matter what the colour of your skin is, your religion or your race. True, the mind may work in a different way depending on the culture you were brought up in, but the real heart of human beings is the same everywhere. Divinity lies within the heart of every man and woman. Go deep inside your hearts during satsang times. You will all surely meet the Divine there.

# Changing the mind

When we are born our minds are clean and pure. It is said that the mind of a child is close to Divinity, yet, very soon, the mind becomes tainted by its surroundings. It is affected by the way one is brought up, one's early experiences in life and what one sees and hears. That is why I always say it is good to bring up children in a loving and spiritual environment. To see portraits of deities or spiritual masters, to see parents devotedly performing pūjās with the family or praying and meditating has a very calming effect on the children and instils peace in them. So how is it that this pure child-mind gets filled with doubt and suspicion? That is the effect of the world and all its illusory ways.

Many adults find that their minds are constantly mistrustful. The mind is always anxious, worrying and doubting everything it comes across. It does not even trust itself and is constantly wavering and changing. The mind generally has a depressive tendency, and it needs lots of things it likes and dislikes to support itself in order to feel that it functions a little efficiently. It relies on many externals – especially drugs, cigarettes and alcohol. Why? Because the mind has no confidence in itself. Even though the mind is a beautiful and perfect instrument, a divine gift, you try to spoil it with all sorts of chemicals. This is stupidity. If you force your mind to like and get addicted to all kinds of awful things, then you cannot let go of those desires. It is better to fight these things in order to go on the spiritual path properly. See how you train your mind – not only do you train it to intake all these chemicals, but to doubt and judge others and also itself! You train it to gossip, to criticize, to dislike, to hate, to want revenge and to desire everything it should not.

So why don't you decide from today onwards to support your poor old mind? Why don't you spring clean it and give it a fresh start, a new, spiritual lease of life? How can you begin?

Firstly, you must really want to change your mind. You must really and truly desire to have a different life, a spiritually inclined one. You can only really do something properly if you have a genuine desire. I believe that most of you have this desire or you would not even be in a position to read these words. You need to have a very strong will to start to reject all the useless and destructive energies that you allowed earlier into your mind. Don't be afraid to step out and jump forcefully onto the spiritual path. I am with you every step of the way. Once you make the first move towards Divinity, then God definitely helps you to travel on that road. The spiritual path itself supports and guides you. If you are lucky, you will meet a spiritual master to accompany you on the path.

So now you are very blessed. You have heard of the true path and you are finding out how to go on it. You have instructions on how to do it and you have someone who knows the way to show you the right direction. The rest is up to you.

Pray to God to give you the strength to start. Pray sincerely. God will definitely answer you with great blessings and give you strength.

Stop fearing. Change fear into strength of mind. Stop hating and disliking. Change those qualities into love. Stop the habits of criticizing and judging. Change them into understanding and encouragement. Stop gossiping. Talk only about divine or good things. Don't wish for revenge on others. Give up everything to God. Ask God to do what is correct.

By consciously following my advice you will learn many things about your real Self and about Divinity.

I bless you all that you may really and truly change your consciousness.

# Spiritual technique

Many of you think that to follow the spiritual path you must use some kind of technique, something that someone successfully followed earlier and through which they became enlightened.

You will find that most great spiritual masters did not use a specific technique. The main reason for their enlightenment was the grace of God or the guru, the realized spiritual teacher. So now you ask me, what is grace? How can we receive grace? Shall we abandon our techniques?

I am not against practising hatha yoga and, by all means, you can follow a particular master. If you wish to practise kriyās and meditation, then you can follow some technique, but my advice to you is to find your own technique with the help of your spiritual teacher.

Forget what the books say. Look deep inside yourself and study yourself.

First, study your own mind and see what its tendencies are. What really interests you spiritually? For example, some people like to take part in rituals very much. When they perform rituals they feel uplifted and concentrated on God. So, if they are genuinely interested, I encourage them by giving them a statue or a lingam. This will be a way for them to meditate easily and to appreciate a form of God. Others say they like meditation and they request a mantra. So I may give them a personal mantra and instruct them how to say that. This is then personally meant for them, not a general instruction. I treat each person as an individual. No two minds are the same. Everyone is different and so I teach each person according to their own tendencies. Of course, there are some general rules and ways that I expect everyone should follow for certain reasons of self-discipline or to facilitate Ashram or Sri Premananda Centre management. That is purely common sense and I hope that everyone is able to understand and comply with simple guidelines that are helpful to everyone. But as far as teaching spirituality goes, I teach everyone in a different way and at a different level.

You are so lucky to have a living spiritual teacher who is ready to help you. You cannot understand the wealth you have gained by having a living guru. I am not talking just about myself. There are a number of great souls teaching in the world right now. Do take advantage of this good fortune and follow their priceless guidance. If your preceptor gives you personal spiritual instructions, you should follow them. Having already experienced every difficulty on the path, he or she knows what to do.

You may have noticed that the lives of saints, when they were young, were never easy. They underwent many difficulties in a very public way to give an example to devotees and aspirants. They demonstrated their devotion and dedication for the sake of others. In the past, Lord Jesus Christ, Lord Buddha, Prophet Mohammed, Sri Ramana Maharishi, Sri Swami Ramdas and his disciple Mother Krishnabai, and, even more recently, Sri Shivabalayogi and Sri Yogi Ramsuratkumar – all underwent severe spiritual practices and many tests and sufferings. See, even today...Swami Premananda! But like all those who immerse themselves in God's divine light and who surrender themselves entirely, I consider everything in my life as God's grace and blessings.

How can you win God's grace? Be absolutely sincere and prepared to give yourself, body and mind, without expectation and unconditionally to the Divine. Pledge to surrender your ego entirely and without demanding anything in return. The more completely you surrender to the Divine, the more God's help and protection surrounds you.

Divinity is the essence of every being in existence. When you realize that great divine energy more and more within yourself by surrendering to it, for what shall you want and fear?

I have said enough. You must experience it yourself. Trust in God. Ask the Divine Mother of the universe to demonstrate her grace. Ask her genuinely, with feeling, and I promise you she will definitely show you. Only, you must really want it.

# Miracles

Religion is simply a gateway. A gateway to faith in God, strong devotion and single-mindedness, understanding, belief in the power of rituals and other such noble concepts.

What is the greatness of Sanātana Dharma? It discourages arrogance, egoism, jealousy and hatred. It is a great source of knowledge on how to attain Self-realization. It advises and demonstrates how to live a cultured life, perform rituals and practise meditation.

Many people come to me with various questions. Some want to research miracles and others want to truly learn spirituality. Many want relief from problems and sorrows. Some desire peace of mind and liberation from the effects of their past actions. Ultimately, all who come only desire one thing – and that is true happiness.

Because of the grace of the Divine, I have the power to generate feelings of peace and happiness in those who come to see me.

If an official visits another person's office, he leaves his calling card to show his credentials and position. Likewise, I show people that I am a representative of God by allowing them to witness certain miracles. These are my visiting cards that make people understand the greatness of God, the ultimate divine power. These small miracles are but a tiny part of God's limitless force.

It is not due to my own wish that lingams manifest from my body and through my mouth during Mahāshivarātri. Do you know that there is a very rare kind of snake, a special cobra, and a precious jewel forms in its mouth from its poison? The poison hardens into a stone in one place in the mouth. This occurs only once in 12 years. The snake puts the stone down only when it goes to eat. In the same way, these lingams form inside my body for nine months. When I bless the devotees, I remove their karmas, their sicknesses, their destructive thoughts, their sufferings and longings. These energies come together in one place inside me and, through the action of a divine flame, they take solid form in the shape of lingams. When they materialize through me, they contain special powers that can take away negative forces from the body and mind.

# Selfless service

Giving help to others without any thought of yourself is an excellent spiritual practice. However, one must know how to give service in a correct way. If you live in the world as a member of a family or as a single person, you may be working and feel you can give donations to charitable or spiritual places. This is one way of giving service. This is a common practice in many religions and for those involved in spirituality.

Others may wish to give their free time to help the poor, the sick and the aged. Whatever your situation, it is always good to give sevā (selfless help) to others. Especially when you go to stay in an ashram, or you take an active part in a spiritual centre, there is no better way of spending your time than by doing some work without thought or expectation of getting something in return. If you work hard without complaining and with a smile on your face, you are a great spiritual example to others, much more so than if you try to tell others what to do on the spiritual path. That is why I always encourage the disciples and devotees in the Ashram to work. You can pray to God, but hands that work hard are as great an offering as lips that genuinely pray. You may belong to a spiritual group or centre – don't talk too much, do something! I always advise you to keep the body busy and the mind still. If you can keep your mind peaceful, full of thoughts of the Divine, and do God's work with your body, that is very, very great.

I like to be a good example to others. If you see the spiritual master and his disciples working selflessly, you will also feel like doing it. If I simply tell others to do this and that, it has little effect.

If you expect others to follow you, first you must put your thoughts and ideas into practice yourself. Talking is not enough. You need to practically do what you say. This is very essential for a spiritual life. When you do selfless service in our Ashram or anywhere else, you forget your ego, yourself, your problems and you think of others and their needs, their difficulties and their sicknesses. If you just idle about the place and talk, talk, talk, you become selfish and you think too much about useless things. You start to talk unnecessarily about others and you lose your peace of mind.

If everyone did one good act of service every day, what a different place this world would be. Most people never do anything at all for others and certainly not for people they hardly know. Most people always want some

42

benefit or they feel they should only help their family and no-one else.

Service to others is a great tradition in India. Our national leaders, such as Mahatma Gandhi, promoted this ideal and it is still part of the heart of the Indian. Sevā is a word known to everyone here. I hope that they will not forget this great heritage and, at the same time, that devotees and friends of Sri Premananda Ashram will realize and promote the value of helping those in need in whatever way they can.

The problem is that everyone tends towards laziness. Most people like to sleep too much. These tendencies will never help you on the spiritual path. Try to overcome them. You need to overcome the mental limits you set for yourself. Stop limiting yourself. You can do anything if you tap into the divine energy source.

I bless you to make more effort, have more patience and progress steadily and surely.

# Gifts from the master

Everything an enlightened soul does has some meaning and a far-reaching effect that the ordinary mind cannot understand or perceive. Because the true master, who is full of wisdom, knows that his movements are all directed and activated from the supreme, divine intelligence, he advises others to reach out to God and experience grace. The more one surrenders to God and the more faith, trust and confidence one has in God, the more help comes and the more one experiences Divinity within oneself.

An important part of the mission given to me by Divinity is to give spiritual objects of worship to devotees. These objects may be materialized from my hands, such as statues or divine forms like yantras, or they may be in the form of lingams that manifest from my body and through my mouth during the Shivarātri festival. In everything I give to you there is an extraordinary divine vibration. It is as if I am giving you a part of myself. By traditionally worshipping in the form of pūjā or simply by just thinking of the object I have given you, the divine energy within it will be activated more and more and you will feel a strong link with God. In more philosophical terms, many spiritual masters talk of jīvātma, the individual soul, and paramātma, the universal soul. Jīvātma must unite with paramātma. The objects I give you truly create a great link between the jīvātma within you and the paramātma, the Universal Consciousness.

I have given a number of manifested lingams to devotees all over the world. If they are using these lingams properly, they are not only quickly uplifting themselves spiritually, but also using the wonderful divine energy contained within the lingams to bless and heal others. If a true master gives any object to an aspirant, there is a tremendous value and benefit in that. The size and appearance of the object are not important. What is important is the spiritual vibration within it.

Not only the statues and lingams I give have great potential. The vibhūti I materialize and give has similar properties. People in the world have faith in allopathic medicine, but this has many side effects. Antibiotics have mental and physical side effects. Vibhūti and lingams do not have such side effects. The energy of these special manifestations works through faith, love and devotion. What is more, they are the creation of Divinity using these same forces. The work done physically, mentally and spiritually by vibhūti, lingams and statues given by me has nothing to do with medicine. They work from the sphere of the soul which governs all levels of well-being. Most people in the world cannot understand this concept because they do not understand the importance of their soul and of trying to realize God. I think that you realize the importance of the soul, because only those who wish to mature spiritually are coming to get advice and help from spiritual masters.

Who is able to help others to heal? Only those who have forged the link between their own soul and the great universal soul we call God. They must reach a certain degree of purity before they can do anything for others.

# Disciples and devotees

Many of you often ask me about renunciation and sannyās. You place much importance on whether you are a disciple or a devotee. You break your head trying to figure out what the difference is between a sannyās disciple and some other kinds of disciples. All these are only words, distinctions and definitions in the mind. However, in order to satisfy you I will give you some guidelines. Asking all these questions is fine for some time, but after a while you need to train yourself to be still in your mind. There will never be an end to your questions. Practise what I say and your questions will all be answered by your own inner realizations.

You cannot categorize everything. You cannot put spiritual progress into different stages – only the spiritual master is able to judge the level of the students. I have given sannyās initiation to some people. This means that they have entered the university of spiritual studies. At this stage, they are trying to give themselves totally to the spiritual life under the guidance of their master. Their aim is to experience complete renunciation. Each and everything they are attached to should be renounced. It is easy to throw away old things that are useless, but it is not so easy to give up your loved ones. That is very difficult. It is not so hard to give up what you do not like.

A genuine sannyāsin must leave behind all likes and dislikes. This means true inner renunciation. It must come from within. You can live in a palace surrounded by luxury, but you should not be attached to any single thing. That is what I mean by genuine or inner sannyās.

Likewise, if you are truly on the spiritual path, it should not matter to you if you are called a devotee or a disciple. You may be my disciple and live far away from me. You may be married and have a family and be carrying out your necessary duties to them, but inside you may be repeating the name of God and thinking constantly of your guru. You may be doing the rituals prescribed for you by your spiritual master in a spirit of joy and devotion. You may always be thinking of ways to help the poor and needy and trying to follow the words of your master in whatever way you can. I would say that such a person is a genuine disciple.

I have many devotees. Their devotion is also pure and sweet. Daily they do their prayers and try to follow my advice on how to cope with their day-to-day problems, their families and, at the same time, go forward on the spiritual path. They are also maturing through their connection with their spiritual master.

If you follow your master's instructions with great feeling and interest, you will progress quickly. Sincerity and right effort in progressing on the spiritual path will definitely be rewarded. Only those who develop such strong feelings towards the Divine can become disciples.

# Divine fragrances

L et us not forget the very simple truths that are the essence of spirituality. It is easy to talk and ask complicated questions but, as I always remind you, the absolute truth is the simplest thing. It is just impossible to define it in words. That is why the truest teaching is passed from master to student in silence, in the form of subtle, uplifting energy.

The sandalwood tree has a very strong, beautiful and overwhelming fragrance. Any tree growing near the sandalwood tree also takes on that same wonderful perfume. Likewise, by being in the presence of divine, spiritual masters, you acquire a little of their 'fragrance'. A true spiritual master has completely lost all attachment to everything. Therefore, through being in the company of such an enlightened person, some of his or her non-attachment will enter your own spirit.

What is the outcome of non-attachment, being unrestricted by likes and dislikes? Non-attachment is important because a pure and unattached mind is free. It is free from the delusions and illusions of the world and all that goes with it. A totally free mind experiences the absolute and unchanging reality we call God. Such experience is simply what is known as mukti in Sanskrit. It is liberation.

There is nothing modern about spirituality. Only the ideas thought up by the human mind and its latest creation and change are known as modern. When people realize that the so-called modern life is totally false, they begin to realize that the spiritual path is the true way. They will realize that only this way can give true peace of mind. Everyone, sooner or later, will set out on the true path.

You can never know when God's grace will engulf you but, if you are broad-minded, when you act selflessly without always thinking, "I, I," when you pray that others will do well in life, when you forgive those who have wronged you... God's grace will provide everything for you. Try to maintain this state of mind.

When you mature and develop devotion for God, the divine energy acts like a magnet. Automatically God will draw you towards him. That same divine magnet will pull out your impure thoughts, ideas and tendencies.

Don't make big problems out of little ones. Try to train your mind to be steady and not to get upset over small, silly matters. Accept that you will always experience good and bad, right and wrong. Duality is the nature of this world. Accept this and don't take everything to heart. Learn from your experiences but stop the mind from going up and down all the time. Practise equanimity. Really practise it. Talk to your mind and stop it from rushing from one emotion to another. By doing this, you will definitely progress in spirituality.

# Accept difficulties
# with a smile

Spirituality belongs to the soul, not to the body. The Tamil word ātma means soul. It is sent to this world, ikam, for a particular purpose. Ātmikam means spirituality. The mind is the instrument of the ātma.

The body is created in order to express the truth of spirituality. It is not necessary to worry about the physical location of the body. It could be in a prison, in a forest, in a cave or anywhere else. The important question is whether or not the body is doing what is correct towards the purpose for which it came.

Fame and ill-fame, ups and downs, happiness and sadness – all these experiences upset and agitate the mind from the time of birth until the moment of death. Because of all these experiences, the mind and body become confused, and the mind forgets the real Self.

The world entangles the ātma in māyā (illusion) by its attractive force, and hence we forget the purpose of our birth and our spirituality.

Since human beings were created there has been a constant conflict between good and evil, between truth and illusion. From the beginning of time, the spiritual ātma has been fighting with great force and will against destructive, negative forces and against māyā for the elevation of the human being towards godliness.

In order to do this, the Supreme Power uses divine incarnations as spiritual instruments. They come in different ways. There are great souls who are called avatārs – incarnations of the sovereign Godhead in a human body. They are mahātmas, great souls and jnānis, those who have attained enlightenment through the path of true knowledge and wisdom. They stood firm on the spiritual path and fought to uplift society spiritually.

They had to face many tests and seemingly impossible difficulties whilst fighting for the truth they stood for, yet they accepted all obstacles with a smile and even-mindedness. Finally, all were successful in their divine work.

Even though the tests and trials undergone by the great souls drowned them and their close associates in a sea of sorrows, they only had the progress of the human race in mind. They always maintained their thoughts at the level of the highest ideal and with the help of spirituality they sacrificed their lives for the service of humanity. Because of their selfless suffering, they have been held in high esteem in the hearts of the future generations as great beings. They overpowered the limitations of time and made humanity understand the truth.

If you think all this over, you will realize that the present-day happenings are not new. You must have the mental capacity to withstand anything! In the test of truth, finally the victory is always for Sanātana Dharma, the ancient and eternal, unchanging laws of nature.

May God bless you all.

# God is inside

You ask so many questions. Questions lead to more questions. There will never be an end to your questions. I don't like to talk too much. I don't like to give your minds too much work because I want your minds to be free. The mind should be free of thoughts. The true Self is that where there is absolutely no thought. Most thoughts pertain to the ego-self. You must be honest and enquire into the true nature of the mind. Once you have put all cares, all thoughts, aside and eliminated your attachments so that you depend solely on God, God himself will bring you everything you need. When the mind is clear and pure, there is real bliss and joy. When thoughts and desires creep in, they bring pain and suffering with them.

God is inside you. Why do you think of God as separate from yourself? Why do you feel you must realize God as something that is not in you? God is inside, and the only way to experience the Divinity within is to first rid yourself of ego, still the mind and reach deep inside to your true Self. By plunging to the depths of your Self, you will experience real and lasting happiness.

A mind that is free from anger and desire is really close to the true Self, which is the Divinity within you. You experience something like the bliss of the Self when your desires are fulfilled, but that sensation is only momentary. Eliminate desire, and you will know true bliss and pure joy.

Do you think that the rich and famous are happy? They may be materially rich but, in truth, they are very poor because they are far from the Self. Your worldly status has no bearing on your spiritual status. I do not look at wealth, position, skin colour or religion. These discriminations are meaningless to me. My devotees and disciples can be from any level of society, rich or poor. They may be intelligent or not so smart. The Divine Mother puts all kinds of people in my charge.

She teaches me, as well as them through me and through the events in my life. If it is your destiny, you will come under my influence and, somehow, you will gain spiritually.

I want you all to develop. All those who are around me now are destined to take part in a great resurgence of spiritual renewal that has been planned by the Divine Mother. Let us humbly and with patience allow her to enact her drama.

You are blessed to be part of these great events.

# Change your qualities

If I am your spiritual teacher I have a lot of work to do. I have to change your mind. Literally. I must change all the qualities in your mind, and I must clean it. I will clean it like a washerman in India beats the dirty clothes to loosen the dirt and then scrubs them with soap. Then he rinses and rinses away the dirt and soap until the clothes are clean and spotless. After removing all the stains and filth, he hangs out the washing to dry in the sun. I have to follow the same procedure to clean your minds.

How can this be done? There are so many ways. I can give you mantras to repeat. I can ask you to perform abhishekams so that you wash away your karmas. I can talk to you. I can ask you to sing bhajans. I can tell you to sit and meditate. When you invite me into your mind, somehow a form of spiritual practice will automatically start. It is a natural process because of the manifest

Divinity in me. Then I will test your progress by giving you small examinations from time to time. Only I know the results, no one else.

Do not think that you have to be by the side of my physical form to learn from me. It is true, by simply looking at you I can speed up your progress. You are very gifted to be in the company of enlightened people because their presence has such a tremendous influence. However, with the master's help, you should be able to develop your own awareness during the course of time. When such an awareness of the guru's presence is felt, then there is no need for physical proximity. That is why I always say you should practise the simple, small sādhana of visualizing me in your mind for a few minutes a day, in solitude. What you can experience inwardly can be far more fulfilling than being close to my physical form. Try, try, try! Sit for some time and see what happens.

I have given many talks and many of my discourses have been written down. These are my spiritual teachings. It would help you very much if you try to follow them. However, a number of devotees and disciples get a little experience but then they do not like to progress because they want to carry on simply doing what they like. They will sit around gossiping and talking about useless things. I always tell you to keep quiet and to follow what I tell you to do. Without thinking or arguing, it is best to do what I tell you. Only then can I truly help you to progress.

In order to teach you properly, there must be receptivity on your part. I am not joking or playing, but I may be testing you. I give simple general instructions that are meant for everyone. But I may give you individual, personal instructions. It is always best to follow them exactly, and then I can guarantee your spiritual success.

# What is truthfulness?

There will be no real peace of mind until you learn to look for the truth. Everything that is impermanent is not the truth. Man's essential problem is that he is foolish enough to regard what is impermanent as if it were everlasting. Everything is transient. All things must pass. So, therefore, what is truth?

Yesterday a man lived, but today he is no more... so the body he made such a fuss of all his life was but illusory and impermanent. What you understood yesterday as true will, most likely, be proved untrue today. What you realize as true today will be proved an illusion tomorrow. So how can you say for sure what is true and what is false? Your own mind is constantly wavering. This is caused by millions of disturbances in the form of immature thoughts. Therefore,

59

how can you know right now, what is true and what is false?

It is best not to try and judge what the truth with regard to others is. It is certainly a grave mistake to judge your spiritual master and to wonder whether he is speaking the truth or not. The enlightened teacher sees everything from a different level. He sees all from a very high position. He is on a different plane of consciousness. Your way of looking at things is very narrow. Only when you grow up spiritually a little more will you lose your blinkered outlook. You will certainly go further on the spiritual path when you train yourself to stop judging and deciding whether your master or anyone else is telling the truth or not.

All your wasted thoughts in judging others should be trained to centre on yourself. It is always better to review yourself. Always correct yourself. Search yourself and see if you are being really honest within or whether you are judging from a biased point of view.

Everyone has a different point of view. So, if you have a mature and flexible mind, you can understand that one person's truth is not another's. That is why it is really foolish to make judgements about others. Can you define what truthfulness is? Can you say any words that are purely truth? Words are only words, after all. Yet, as far as spirituality is concerned, the words of the master are full of power. One should understand the nature of one's enlightened master. There is a famous Sanskrit shloka which explains that the words of the guru are like a holy mantra because of their extraordinary power.

The problem is that the modern disciples do not realize the value of having an enlightened teacher. It is an extremely rare gift to find such a master. Do not waste your time with your precious gift of a true teacher by trying to analyze his every word to see if it matches your immature idea of what truth is. It would be far better to search for the truth inside you.

Do away with all the impermanent rubbish-thoughts in your head.

Stop judging everyone and everything.

Relax, and accept what is.

Be still, and you will know what truthfulness is.

# The problem of jealousy

What does your spiritual master want? He wants his disciples and devotees to be perfect. He wants them to be true and, above all, sincere in their search for the Divine. He especially wants them to be without jealousy. He would like them to be like little children with pure minds, ready to realize the truth.

Jealousy stops you from progressing spiritually.

If your nature has changed so much that you are free from envy, then it is really a sign that you are advancing spiritually. Jealousy leads one to hurt others. Not only that, jealousy eats away good virtues and spoils the mind. It is even said in Hinduism that Lakshmi, the Goddess of wealth, will go away from one who is envious. One who is walking the spiritual path will certainly leave it if he is always thinking enviously about the good fortune or status of others.

Many shishyas (spiritual students) like to feel that they are close to the guru, but I always stress that one must be close to God and not to the physical form of the teacher. Thinking that you should always be with the master and that he should always give you attention will lead you to being jealous if he does not speak with you. You will always be observing how long he talked with others and you will spend your time watching his every move. Ultimately, you will forget your true goal, which is progression on the spiritual path.

Jealousy is especially a big problem for ladies. I am not saying that men do not have jealousy, but it is very noticeable in women. If I spend more time talking with one lady, the other ladies are not happy. Each one feels that she is the one who should be given special treatment. Secretly, some ladies would like the other women to be sent away so that there would be less competition for them.

Why? Because they lack self-confidence. Deep inside they are frightened. They always feel they need someone to support them and they are used to that. They want a partner, and they expect that the guru should be their permanent partner and not pay much attention to others. Men, however, are not so concerned with making a permanent relationship. They think of relationships in a more temporary way.

If women can destroy their jealous tendencies, then their great qualities of constancy and faithfulness will be a wonderful asset on the spiritual path. Women must first pass the age-old test of getting rid of their jealousy of other women.

The master knows the maturity and sincerity of his students. He can see into your past, present and future lives. The master knows much more than that also, but words cannot express how much he understands about you.

Work on yourself. Remove jealousy. If you feel jealous, think positively about that person. Think of their good qualities and pray for them. Always think good things and stop thinking and talking negatively. Think of your master whenever you feel jealous. He will definitely help you through his divine energy and power of purity.

# The spiritual path and married people

The spiritual path is for everyone. It is common property, and it is not meant for one particular kind of person. There are many ways of practising spirituality and, whatever your life situation, you can follow the teaching of your spiritual master.

In traditional Indian literature, married people are called householders. I have many householder devotees and disciples. When the destined time arrives, whether you are married or not, your spiritual master will come into your life. A married person with a family has much opportunity to grow on the spiritual path because he or she is always confronted with so many different experiences and responsibilities. Therefore, if you are on the spiritual path and you have a family, you should realize that this way of life is necessary for you to grow and mature. The circumstances and events you experience help you to develop the qualities necessary to progress further.

Above all, you should always try to be selfless and consider the feelings of your partner. That is a lesson in denying the ego-self. Kindness and consideration are the key points here. If your partner is also on the spiritual path and you happen to have the same teacher, you are indeed greatly blessed. You can support and help each other on your spiritual journey. At the same time, you can cultivate non-attachment by accepting the actions and faults of your partner without getting angry or allowing yourself to experience negative reactions. All that happens to you in life is an experience to teach you on the spiritual path. Once you have come under the influence of the spiritual master, always learn from each experience.

Many married devotees start their relationship with the guru because they have family problems. In fact, it is these problems that lead them to the guru who helps them by giving advice on how to overcome the problems. The devotee should understand that the guru's advice is not of this world. It is advice that comes through the guru's divine wisdom. It is practical and based on his knowledge of the future of the devotee. By constantly referring to the guru with his problem, the devotee develops confidence in the guru. This is the beginning of the spiritual path.

Very often a strong link is established between me and all the members of a family. For many, I am part of their family although I am not physically present. In this way, the whole family live with some spiritual energy constantly surrounding them. I guard them and help them. I come to them when they call for my help.

The trust that householder disciples have in me is the foundation of strong spiritual faith. I encourage them to grow on the path of bhakti (devotion), of faith and love for the Divine. Their spiritual practice is to seek the blessings of the master and always feel his presence and all-encompassing, all-forgiving and all-knowing, loving bliss.

# What is grace?

I often bless you saying that you have my grace. So now you all ask me, "What is grace?" Grace is very difficult to understand with the logical mind. Only those who are sensitive spiritually can feel grace and its action.

In India, it is commonly said that only the grace of the guru can give the disciple liberation. This is because the spiritual path is not an easy one. However, with the gift of divine energy from the guru, all obstacles can be overcome. What are the obstacles? They are all in your mind, your personality and your ego. All these things have to be brought into control or got rid of. A spiritual master who has fully developed can give you the willpower to stand up to these old, negative tendencies that will try to turn you away from the path of true spirituality.

Do not think it is very easy to win grace. In order to earn grace, you must be genuine and have a sincere aspiration to go forward a little on the path of spirituality. Even simply calling out to God to help you is a big step forward for many people. Many devotees have problems of all kinds, and so they call out for God's help, or they write to me and ask me to ask God on their behalf. So this is a great step. Because of their request, definitely grace will descend on them in some form, but they may not realize it at once. They may not realize at all that they have received grace because they are not yet in a position to feel the divine energy that helped them.

The nature of a real spiritual master is pure compassion for all beings. Even if you have not asked for help and you are heading for a fall, the grace of the guru may shower on you. Even if the master shouts at you and seems to be angry about something, he is showering you with grace.

Do not imagine that only sweet and seemingly kind words give grace. I often say, "Guru's curses are his kisses!" When he seems angry the guru has even more spiritual energy. Yet, it is difficult for you to understand the ways of the true teacher and how and when he grants grace. He seems like a small child – he will go to some people spontaneously and bless them. Yet he will not go for some time to others who are calling him – or he may not go at all. The guru knows who is sincere and who is not. He also knows exactly the correct time to shower his grace for the maximum spiritual effect.

All these things happen naturally through the guru. Don't imagine that he is planning everything. He simply acts according to the will of the Divine. Never forget that the guru is the channel for divine energy that is totally natural and spontaneous. Try to continually keep yourself in tune with the divine energy by being flexible and adaptable.

Try to always think of God and divine things in order to receive grace. You need to be always ready. If you are not ready, fresh and pure-hearted, thinking of the Divine – when the divine energy wants to suddenly descend on you – how can it enter you if you are not prepared?

There must be some unity between the guru and disciple or devotee for the grace to work fully. Then the grace flows continually. So think often of your spiritual master. Always imagine that he is with you. Then you will always follow his advice because you will feel that he is with you all the time and his grace, which is the grace of God, will be part and parcel of your every second. You will swim in a sea of grace.

# Delete the old movie

In spirituality there will come a time when you know that this whole world is false. You are always seeing the same old picture, the same old movie. Finally, you must be fully convinced that this whole world and its relationships are like an old movie that you have seen over and over again on the television.

Ultimately, you realize that there is really nothing truly of interest for you in this material world. If you realize that and understand a little of the concept of what spiritually really is, then you will seriously start to walk the true path. If you truly understand this through your own experience, not merely through others telling you, that is more than enough to start out on the spiritual way.

You will experience all the ups and downs, difficulties, problems, sufferings and tensions of the world. After experiencing all these ups and downs and inner pain and sorrow, because of the impermanence of everything around you, you will suddenly reach out for the true reality.

Then you may think, "Ah well, this is the end of it and now I will come to the spiritual life." But then you have to go through even more ups and downs so that you really know that the worldly life is false. Finally, after repeatedly experiencing this old movie, you will find a blank screen. Now you are finding a little peace of mind. You watched this movie so many times that you are absolutely fed up with it, and you throw it away. Yet still, the desire and attachment for the old habits will persist.

You think you have to sleep on time...you complain bitterly because you have some pain...you think everything is difficult or a big problem for you...you must eat on time and drink this and that. You have taken hold of all these habits and attached yourselves to them so strongly...what to do?

Be flexible and adjust. Be patient and strong. Be able to adjust at any minute to what is happening around you. Spiritual life is spontaneous, like death. Can you say at what minute you are going to die? Likewise, spiritual realization will come upon you suddenly and without warning. That's why it is important to train your mind to be open to accept and adapt to any circumstances.

You are used to fixed routines and doing things in a certain way. So your first enemy on the spiritual path is your worldly background. That's why, when you are setting out in the spiritual life, you need to change the environment you are in. You were very flexible and accepting when you were a child. You need to become like that once more.

After constantly training the mind to be open and cleaning it at every possible moment, the old movie will be erased. You will be free, like an innocent child. Just the blank screen will be there, but no movie will be showing anymore.

Now, can you understand what I am trying to say? I will leave you to think about it. Finally, you must also kick out that blank screen.

# Living alone

I am not telling you all that you must live alone. Yet it is of very great benefit if you can spend some part of your life living in solitude. At least, if you cannot do that, spend some time each day, or even each week, when you deliberately take time out on your own to be quiet.

During this time, do some spiritual activities or simply just 'be'. It is a natural thing for someone to take time to be alone. Some people do it by gardening or by doing some other peaceful and natural activity. Some like to walk in the countryside, in a place away from others. In the Ashram, some people go to sit and meditate on the big rocks.

What does it mean to be truly alone? It means to be for some time without attachments and thoughts and to reach deep inside and communicate with your Self. Many spiritual teachers encourage spending some time in solitude. However, many people are really afraid to be on their own. They always want some company and something to occupy the mind. They don't really want to know themselves or face their faults.

If you want to grow spiritually, it is not much use socializing by talking all kinds of rubbish with everyone. Most people like to chat and gossip. Think carefully, if you allow everyone to come to your house and you listen to all kinds of talk, your mind will become poisoned. Yes, this kind of unnecessary, often untrue and unkind talk is like a poison in the mind that spoils your spiritual practices. You should be very aware of this. If nobody is able to invade your mind, there will be no poison there. But, if you allow everyone to come and talk, talk, talk and say all kinds of garbage to you, your mind will get confused and full of nonsense.

Please don't allow your mind to become a rubbish bucket. If you let it become a bucket full of filth, how can it be a vessel for pure grace at the same time? This is common sense. You must be clean in order to receive good and pure things. Why waste your time cleaning up your mind and keeping it free ready for someone else to dump their nonsense in it? After some time, that rubbish will go bad and rot. Finally, it will putrefy and give off a dirty smell, which is of no use to anyone.

If you talk with others, it is better to talk only about good things in a positive way. Make your life happy and make these times good times. Do not destroy these good times. Life should be joyful. Realize the greatness of the spiritual path that you always tell me you want to follow. Why spoil your spiritual life by talking about the madness in the world and the silly things that people do and say? Gossip is usually about silly, silly, little matters.

Speak of necessary things. If you want to go to a higher stage of evolution and if you genuinely want to develop your mind, first of all learn how to live alone. If two women live together, they will certainly gossip and there will be no end to it. They will get stuck in one place talking.

It is a gift to be alone most of the time. Not only that, if you see that someone is living a spiritual life in solitude, do not go and spoil it for them. Visit them if you must, but do your best to help them. Do not leave poison with them and so destroy their spiritual life.

When you are in solitude, it is easier to find your own ideas on how to be spiritual. Some people think they know everything and they like to give their ideas to others. They think they are doing a great favour by advising others, but actually they are mostly talking without knowing anything. Such people push others into a ditch. They put them down. It can happen to anyone. That is why I advise you to be alone so that you can think of higher things with deep concentration. Think of your spiritual teacher and ask for his grace to guide you and show you how to be free.

# Helping relatives understand your path

When starting out on the spiritual path it does no harm to do a bit of research about it. It is better to try and find out about it from people who really know the subject. Get good advice from genuinely spiritual people and those who have thoroughly practised and gained true results themselves.

People who are close to you in the world very often cannot advise you. Sometimes your parents may be spiritual people, and they may understand and encourage you. Quite often, however, your relatives and old friends will not understand your choice of learning about the truth and your real Self, and they may discourage you or even make fun of you. If you listen to them and try to do what they want all the time, you can never go on the spiritual path. The problem is that they do not believe in this, and neither do they understand. However, some may have involved themselves a little in this way of life. They may have enquired about it and understood the spiritual way to some extent.

Those who are against this life are very involved in the world, and they have neither the time nor the inclination to follow the spiritual path. They are simply living the way their parents lived. They know how to get a job, how to have children and live a mundane life until they die. The spiritual life is something far beyond their understanding. If you tell them what I explain to you, they will think that both you and I are mad. The only way that can help them understand is if they get some kind of deeper experience. If you explain to your spiritual master that you want your parents and friends to understand you, he will definitely help, and the Divine will show them something extraordinary that will help both them and you. Realize that it is very difficult to make anyone else understand spiritual truths. First, try to realize something yourself.

Each one thinks that only he or she knows something about life. Everyone has a different concept of how life should be. Whatever you believe it to be, that is really also not true. What worldly people feel life actually is – that is a complete falsehood and hypocrisy. A material life is really a superficial life. You reach the true depths of life when you go inside and search for the truth yourself.

Think about this. You may be smiling. That is, your mouth is smiling, but internally you are not smiling. A really spiritual person will smile in his or her mind with devotion and love. They will be like this all the time. The people of the world cannot do this. They will often feel negative emotions such as anger, jealousy, impatience and desire. How, then, can you take advice from the people in the world regarding your own, very special, sacred inner life? Take that advice only from a proven spiritual master, if you are lucky enough to have contact with such a master.

Yet, still, I will always advise you to honour your parents, your family and your friends. Treat them kindly with love and respect. Do your duty – but keep your mind free and surrender it to the Divine.

# Are you ready for my spiritual push?

**M**any of you complain to me that the spiritual life is hard because you experience a series of emotional and inner upheavals. When you come under the influence of strong, divine energy such disturbances will definitely happen. You are asking the Divine to change and purify you in all respects and so, naturally, you will feel it at every level. Change is always hard. When the spiritual energy pervades you, and you are undergoing constant transformation, it becomes difficult to adjust. But that is your training – patience, adjustability, forbearance, strength of mind, development of the will. How can you change unless you exercise all these qualities?

Grace is there. Divine grace will help you to effect these changes, but you must expect that you will undergo tensions and worries on your spiritual path.

I love you all very much. I am not angry with any one of you. To me, you are all my children. When I see you going through inner turmoil, maybe fighting with each other and feeling sad, I observe everything but I do not let myself get involved. Therefore, I do not feel unhappy about your upsets. Yet I do care, and I do something about it by calling for God's grace to help you.

For me to do that effectively, you must first call for me to help you. I hear all your prayers. Do not doubt it. I help you always. If you give me the responsibility of looking after your problem, I will definitely help you and carry out the duty you have given to me. After telling me your problem in your prayers, in a letter or in person, you do not really need to remind me. The best result will happen in the time it has to happen.

At the same time, if you ask me to teach you spirituality, I expect that you will put into practice what I say. If you say you sincerely want to progress, I will really push you on to the spiritual path. I will not just prod you with my little finger; I will shove you on to the path with both hands!

Before pushing you, I will first warn you that I am going to give you a big, spiritual push...so be strong so that you do not fall. When I warn you, you must brace yourself and be ready for it. So now I am telling you that I am going to push you...push you...push you. I am telling you well in advance because I want you to be ready and I want to make sure that you are not going to fall. I am giving you prior warning that I am about to push you all headlong into real spirituality.

How can you get ready? If you go on a journey, how do you ready yourself? You put on clean clothes, you put on make-up, spray perfume and do your hair. That is getting ready for a worldly journey. For a journey on the spiritual path, first you must clean up your mind. Clean out your ego and desires. Take these out of yourself. Put them outside. When you go into the world you have to put these things inside. Otherwise, it is difficult to live there. Unfortunately, if you live a worldly life you need to understand lies and hypocrisy. The world is full of these, so you need to experience them. When you are seriously going on the spiritual path, put such things out – and keep them out.

# A pure mind

In the Tamil language, my mother tongue, the word for purity is parisuttam. It is a very rich word full of meaning and feeling. In the normal, modern world, purity is not something that is discussed or is considered of value, but in spirituality it has the greatest worth because only a completely pure mind can reach the feet of God.

Normally, the mind is totally involved in the material world. It always attaches itself to unnecessary things. It is constantly disturbed by tense and anxious thoughts. It attaches itself to thoughts of the past, what is going on now and what might happen in the future. It is full of ideas of what it wants. It is ceaselessly wanting and desiring. It demands not only normal things such as food and drink, but all kinds of pleasures. It wants to be constantly fulfilled. The demands of the egoistic mind are never, ever satisfied.

You need to face up to the fact that in order to have a spiritual life you need to begin to purify yourself. It is an ongoing process that does not end until you attain realization. You will have to clear up everything that is in your mind. Your harmful qualities, thoughts and selfish ideas will have to be cleaned up, and your entire way of thinking has to change. This is the meaning of making the mind pure.

It can be difficult to do it practically because there are many, many problems to be faced in daily life. Yet it can be done, especially under the guidance of a genuine spiritual teacher.

First, you need to understand yourself in order to purify yourself. Review the processes of your mind and understand why it is going in the opposite direction from spirituality. Having diagnosed what is wrong with it you can slowly bring it under control.

You must understand that the mind is impure because it is used to doing things in a certain way. For example, it may always want to smoke or admire a lady because of her beauty. It got used to that. That is the mind's age old habit. So first you realize that smoking is bad for your health and for your mental state. Then you understand that your admiration of the beautiful woman will lead you to further unnecessary thoughts about her. Now you can start to control yourself. Reduce the cigarettes and convince yourself you want to be independent from them. Think of the woman as your own sister or mother. This is the way to purify your mind. Substitute your not so nice tendencies with helpful ones. Practise good thoughts and ideas and don't allow your mind to run away with you through useless imaginings.

Always remember that you cannot become mature without becoming pure. One can also say that purifying the mind is like losing weight. You must eventually lose your negative tendencies, leaving only the helpful ones. In this way, you will have a light, free and independent mind.

Keeping your mind free and clear is a constant practice. Give up jealousy and desire. Especially watch egoism, the feeling that 'I' want everything, 'I' can do everything and 'I' know everything. Conceit and arrogance are two naughty people who have been having a good time living inside you. Throw these awful two out. The minute you throw them out, they will try and creep back into you again. Keep on taking them out and ask them to mind their own business. If you tell them often enough, they will listen to you. Your mind and your Self are very good people. Egoism and arrogance are your enemies – keep them and all their friends (jealousy, desire and so on) at a big distance.

# Anti-virus spirituality

One can say that this is Swamiji's speciality. One of my favourite sayings is, "Don't disturb your mind unnecessarily." Why do you allow everything to come into your mind? Whenever anything is going on, you immediately allow it to enter you and upset you.

To stop everything from coming into your mind, build a strong fence around it. Your mind is like a garden, and I have planted a precious seed of spirituality in it. Protect that seedling and allow it to grow. Stop all the animals from coming to eat it and trampling on it. Why should you show your lovely little plant to everyone? They will look at it with scornful or envious eyes, and some may plot to destroy it. Keep it fenced off until it is a strong and healthy young tree. Give it plenty of water and fertilizer when it needs it. Be aware of what it needs. Negative tendencies find it very difficult to penetrate such a strong barrier. Confusion and sorrow cannot survive the brilliant light of pure love. Jealousy hates happiness and runs away from it.

Love everyone and be kind to everyone. A pure heart becomes immune to outside disturbances. Be kind to your mind and explain to it gently what is right and wrong, just like I am trying to do to you.

The ancient sages always gave the example of the young tree and likened it to the development of the human being on the great divine path. These days we must use modern comparisons to make the young generation understand what we are trying to say.

Let us say that your mind is like a computer. Therefore, we can assume that most of your minds are computers that have different kinds of viruses. So you need to install an anti-virus program to clean up your personal computer (your mind). Having removed the virus, you should not run the old diseased program disk in your clean mind. You should first clean it up, or better still, install a newer, more efficient program which is suited to your new spiritual needs. Still, you need to check the computer daily to see if a virus has jumped into your program from outside.

The computer virus is like the rotten thought that finds its way into your mind, wends its path into your heart and stays there. It will stay in your heart like a stain and work itself into your body and become part of you. That is why you have to immediately clean it up after understanding what kind of virus (impure thought) it is.

Find out how it got there and why it is staying there.

Knowing these things, you can effectively clean it out of your system.

This is real self-enquiry and discrimination.

The word *purity* is only a word. You cannot become pure just by talking and saying the words. You have to do everything actively and practically. We can actively practise purity and put it into action.

It is easy to say nirvāna, moksha or liberation but how can we have this transcendent experience? Drop negative thinking, anger and other such feelings that spoil your divine life. Understand the internal politics that go on in your mind. Understand, control and eliminate them.

Start now. Don't wait! Time is short. I am here to help you. All you have to do is ask me.

# Distance is no barrier

You might think that because you are physically far away from me, you cannot be in contact with me. You fear that because I live at such a distance from you, I am not aware of you. You feel that you are not close or dear to me because of that distance. So let me clear up your doubts and fears about this.

Divine energy is something that is able to transcend any barriers of time and space. However far away you may be physically, the divine energy is able to reach you in an instant. You are not aware of it, but sometimes it is this divine energy that makes you think of me. Sometimes I am wishing that you should think of me and you do so. Whenever I think of you, immediately, without your knowledge, my energy comes into you to help you.

It is natural for a spiritual master to think of those whom he teaches and guides. He thinks of his pupils as if they were his own children, wherever they are. Is it not natural for a mother and father to think of their children? If you take one step forward towards me and the spiritual gifts that I have to offer you, I take a number of steps towards you.

Even if you get tired of me and think that you want to leave me and not think of me anymore, that does not automatically mean that I will step back from you. I do not walk away from you, but I stay in the same position and still go on thinking of you, praying for you and protecting you from danger and unseen forces. I stay in the same place and do not change because I have a steady mind and a true heart. I know what is best for you.

It is divine power that is working through me, so when you keep me in mind and follow the principles for the spiritual path that I have given, you are getting closer to God. I do not want you to try and come closer to me physically. My body is impermanent, and so is yours. You might ask questions and we may laugh together, and I might discuss your problems and solve them, but ultimately my aim is to make you realize God, which you cannot do by always being around me physically.

To realize God, you must associate with me spiritually and, in that case, distance is no problem. In fact, distance can help. You must realize the truth that is within you. I am not asking you to leave your home, partner or family. I ask you to follow spiritual teachings and find the truth inside. Realize that I am always with you.

I live in your heart. In order to discover that I am in your heart, you need to develop a certain amount of trust and belief in me and in my teachings. You may not understand me immediately. There is a world of difference between your mentality and mine, and that is why you cannot straightaway grasp what I tell you. Your life is centred on YOU whereas my life is centred on GOD. That is the great difference between us.

I do not think anything is mine. Everything is the will and play of God, and I am only an instrument in his hands. By the grace of God, I make you less selfish and more inclined to the spiritual, selfless life.

It is God's will that he has made this body of mine full of divine energy. If you have a problem and you think of me, the solution comes very quickly. Even if a third party prays to me on behalf of someone else, the divine energy helps that person. I can tell you so many things... but it is better if you try it out and see the results for yourself.

# Experience the answers

Divinity has given me a great gift. I am using this gift to point something out to you. I want you to simply understand and truly know that Divinity exists. I know that because I see Divinity and I perceive this Supreme Consciousness as pervading all reality.

I enjoy Divinity directly and personally. I think you can all understand that and you see it in my behaviour, my expression and my happiness, whatever my personal circumstances may be. When you look in my face and hear my words, I hope that you gain a little of the bliss that I have been given by God.

With this great gift that I have, it is possible for me to get rid of your problems and all the difficulties that you face in your life and to cure your diseases. I am really concerned that you should have faith in the divine power. It is easy for me to help you if you have belief in Divinity. Then, what I say will come to pass in your life easily and quickly.

You may have to live an ordinary life with a family and carry out your responsibilities towards your children. That certainly does not mean that you are forbidden to walk on the spiritual path. It is only necessary to keep one major thought in your mind. Whatever you do in life, have faith in God and always think of God.

Change your attitude towards life. Change from a life desiring constant enjoyment to a life in pursuit of something eternal, everlasting and worthwhile. We are not going to live for hundreds of years. So try not to waste your time during your short life. The most important qualification you need is a spiritual master.

You are very fortunate that you can ask me your many questions. I have answers for all the questions in your minds. I do not just have words as answers to your questions. I can make you experience the answers. I can show you God, and I can make you realize and understand God. I say this with confidence because I have known, understood and experienced the great, divine power. I did not learn anything from books.

I am not interested in guiding you on a false path or a useless search. I will certainly never send you in the wrong direction. I would never do such a thing to you. I want you to understand and experience what I have known.

Some ignorant people, who are too lazy to try and understand, may say that God is the creation of the human mind. The opposite is true. The human race itself has been created by divine power. We finite beings have been brought forth by the great, infinite power of God, yet we are still unable to perceive the truth of the existence of his omniscient and all-powerful presence.

I end this talk with some practical advice. Always think that you are good people. Everyone in this world is good, only their backgrounds and environment change them and send them in the wrong direction. Live in a suitable environment and slowly your mind will improve. Don't think too much. Don't be so suspicious. Too much questioning leads to more doubts. Above all, don't ask *why* too much...the why question leads to confusion and reduces your faith. Search deep inside yourself.

All is within you.

Trust me, and I will show you the way. However, you must make a strong and sincere effort.

# Who will realize God quickly?

How much devotion do you have? You will mature in your spiritual life according to how much you feel for God. Only if you are very anxious to reach God will you grow accordingly. You may have been practising for five, ten, twenty or more years but you cannot say at which point you will reach the ultimate goal of realization. In your minds, you still have possessiveness, jealousy, pride, ego, desire for name and fame, selfishness and other adverse qualities that prevent you from realizing the Self.

Who will achieve realization quickly? Those who concentrate their minds on God or their spiritual master, who want nothing for themselves, who surrender themselves totally without any reservations, who desire no worldly thing but only the grace of God. Only when one has attained such a high state of mind can one explain what one has realized in the spiritual life.

How can you reach such a spiritual state? By daily meditation, by keeping company with spiritual people, by singing devotional songs and performing devotional rituals, such as abhishekam and pūjās. The mind becomes pure and peaceful when life is dedicated to giving selfless service to one's fellow beings. Through all these practices one attains peace of mind.

The guru and disciple relationship is very important for spiritual advancement. A true guru has walked every step on the spiritual path. He or she knows every problem and tendency of the student's mind. The guru knows you better than you know yourself. Through his divine power he can see your natural tendencies and how best to correct you.

I want to give you all a special message. Try to follow this advice as best you can. You will find that you will progress very quickly.

If a person talks badly of another, he will not do so in that person's presence, but behind his back. You all say you want to live in harmony with others. If that is really true, why do you always see their faults? Do you think that you are a fit person to correct them? My best advice to you is to observe their faults – but to ignore them. You yourself have so many faults, yet you only see the mistakes made by other people. So who is going to point out your mistakes? Try to correct yourself first before accusing someone else. Call on your guruji to help you go in the right direction.

My best blessings are with you to become perfect in this lifetime.

# Surrender!

Y ou always ask me what it means to surrender. You ask me so many questions and it is easy for me to reply. Sometimes, however, I also question...what is the use of answering? But in my heart the divine energy we call the Beloved Mother of the Universe tells me to answer you, and so I immediately do so. I cannot think of questioning her because I have surrendered myself entirely to her. She is God, the highest, the Absolute.

Surrender is not slavery. When you talk of surrender, don't think in terms of demeaning or lowering yourself. You should think, "I am surrendering at God's feet." When you say "God" think of the concept of God in the highest and most reverent manner you possibly can. When I think of God, I worship with the greatest of respect and in a deep, purely spiritual way. If you constantly feel that you are with God and your thoughts are always at that supreme level then really trying to surrender is not necessary. It is automatic because your energy and the divine energy are one.

In the process of going towards true surrender, the mind's complicated thought processes become untangled. Then you can clearly see what has to be removed from within you. First surrender your egoism, then your useless and deceptive pride and then your unbearable arrogance. Instead of thinking, "I, I, I", forget your ego-self and think of the great source, the pure mother energy that activates you and every living being in the universe. Realize the greatness of this force. What is there that she cannot do? Place yourself in her arms and ask her to purify you, ready to receive the truth.

After all, what is it that you are all striving for and longing for so much? You are all struggling to reach the divya shakti, the divine energy, which is your true nature. Surrender is not something we do for selfish reasons, with an ulterior motive or to gain something. To honestly and sincerely surrender, you need certain qualities. You should have a pure and devotional mind. It is quite something to truly have such a mind. Even when you reach that stage of your spiritual life, you will only begin to understand the extent to which you have surrendered yourself.

How to surrender? To start with you need to have some faith in God, the Supreme Being (or whatever way you like to think of that which is within us and beyond us). To surrender you need to have faith in the Divine in some way. In Tamil, we say that the Divine is paramporul, which means the greatest and highest thing in existence.

Through your striving and devotion you will win the divine grace to proceed further on the path. Lastly, but of great importance, you need to trust in your spiritual master fully. Whatever the master instructs you to do, you must understand that there is a reason for it. Try and understand these reasons if you can. If you cannot understand, don't find fault because of your lack of comprehension. Have the confidence that whatever happens is for your own good and develop such a positive way of thinking.

Divine souls, to surrender is important. You want to know the truth of life and enjoy great peace. By letting go of unwanted thoughts, you are freeing yourself of excessive, misleading thinking and you will reach the truth. Only by doing this can you start to know surrender.

# Shakti

What is the primeval force that motivates the universe? What existed at the beginning of time? A divine vibration, a tremendous, indescribable force. In the ancient Sanskrit language, it was called shakti. Later on, people called this power 'Divine Mother' and gave it many different names, because all in existence has come from it.

There are extraordinary vibrations in the elements also. Hindu scriptures refer to water as Ganga Devī and the River Ganges as Mother Water. They call the earth Bhūmi Devī, the Mother Earth, and fire is known as Agni Devī, Mother Fire. That from which all life emanates is called Mother by the Hindus. As the early people developed, they worshipped the earth, the rivers, seas and fire and referred to them as Mother Goddesses.

If you go beyond the name and forget the form, then that pure force is shakti.

Now imagine me, Swamiji. Take away my name and form and think I have no name and no body, but still there is a consciousness, an extraordinary living vibration. That is shakti. That is Mother. You must train yourself to understand and perceive shakti, the divine force. Most people will perceive zero, nothing, because they cannot think beyond name and form.

Hindus worship fire through yāgams, fire ceremonies. We understand the purifying force of water through abhishekams, ceremonies of ritual bathing of the forms of the Gods. We worship Mother Earth through meditation. Different types of electricity, divine currents and vibrations run through the earth. Likewise, the same forces run through our bodies during meditation.

During meditation the ancient peoples repeated Aum, the sacred syllable representing the primordial sound of creation. Just as this force is called ādi parāshakti (the original supreme energy), it is also called Aum shakti. When one repeats Aum inwardly or outwardly it arouses the shakti known as kundalinī within our bodies. This energy rests at the base of the spine. By repeating Aum with true feeling and concentration, we can arouse the divine forces in our bodies and bring them up towards the crown of the head. This process should be done carefully and only with the guidance of a genuine master. By continuing sincere spiritual practice in this way, the sound and extraordinary vibration of Aum will mingle with the blood in our bodies. Through the slow breathing necessary to perform Aumkar (chanting of Aum), Divinity circulates with the blood throughout the body. It comes to the heart and makes it beat with a divine vibration. Aum should circulate inside you. That is why you should not rush when chanting Aum. The deep and long breath in between the verbal chanting of Aum is of most importance.

Remember that every concept in existence is contained in the primeval force of shakti. She is everything, and she can do everything for you. You have nothing to fear or to worry about if you worship the Mother force. Mother always does her motherly work, even more so than a human mother.

Worship the whole world as Mother by serving her and all her dear children.

# Golden words

*You say that God is one, yet there is truth in all religions...can you explain this?*

Water is water. You may prefer to drink it chilled. Another may like it hot and yet another with orange, tea or coffee. That depends on the taste and culture of the drinker and his or her environment. People have different preferences but the essential and common ingredient, the water, does not change. The various tastes and inclinations of humanity are the many religions. Christianity, Jainism, Islam, Buddhism, Hindu Sanātana Dharma...these are the different flavours. Even within these religions, every individual thinks and feels from an entirely distinct and separate standpoint. And the water? The water is none other than God, the bedrock and support, the number one essential ingredient of most religions.

*You say that celibacy is best for the spiritual path, but you have many married devotees. Do you expect them not to have sex?*

Desire of the body for sex is temporary and is satisfied in five or ten minutes. I am in a difficult position to say these things when so many of my devotees are married. There are also many young people who want to marry who take notice of my advice. Sex is normal and natural for married people. I will never say that they should not do that, but I must say the truth that the highest life is that of brahmacharya, perfect self-control in body and mind. Indeed, it is a path fraught with difficulty, but it is the true way to the highest spirituality.

In order to achieve self-control one needs to persevere with a strong will, patience and determination. The fruits are indeed great – permanent wisdom, divine bliss and immortal, endless happiness. The ultimate pleasure of sex is over in a few seconds. Logically speaking, where is the comparison? You must decide for yourself if you want to practise celibacy of body and mind. It is a very serious step in the life of a spiritual aspirant. You should never upset or spoil the life of your marriage partner because of your decision. You have a duty to your partner.

You decide. I will certainly never force anyone to be celibate.

*I heard you advising some people regarding their spiritual practices. They seemed very advanced. Even though I have been practising for one year, it seems to me I have not progressed so much. What can I do?*

Some of you have come to me over the years and you think you are very highly developed. I will not tell you otherwise. I may seem to agree with you so as not to upset or disappoint you.

Your problem is that you think you must do everything in a hurry. If we lay down house foundations and then immediately build the walls, will our building last? No, it will first crack and then tumble down. We must leave the foundations sometimes for a very long time to give a perfect, rock-solid base for our future building.

Likewise, you should realize that you are only at the beginning of spirituality. In fact, you have not even started yet. You are only laying the foundations for a spiritual life. Don't give up. You will progress steadily.

*I live in the city. It is not a spiritual environment. What can I do?*

Wherever you are it does not matter. In any place you live, try to create a spiritual environment. This is helpful to changing yourself. A spiritual environment inspires good thoughts, actions, right living and charity. In these ways you can train yourself to change your life and go in a divine direction, wherever you live.

# Overcoming common problems

So you want to know how to have faith? Faith in what? If you want to have faith in your spiritual teacher, it is not necessary that you should research and understand him or her too much.

Spiritually elevated souls can sometimes seem a little strange to worldly people. A worldly person sees things from a very narrow-minded point of view and so it is impossible for an ordinary person to see or understand the point of view of a spiritually mature person. Spiritually developed people do not really expect others to follow them or understand their every word and action. They are not even worried if others have no faith in them.

They live only to show the truth to others.

Some people say to me, "Oh, Swamiji, today you say this and tomorrow you will say another thing. To me you advised one thing, and to Raja you said another. How can I understand you?" Does Mother Earth have the same reaction with the millions of plant species growing in her all over the planet? No. She feeds each species in a different manner according to that plant's own characteristics. She knows exactly how to nurture the mango tree so it will produce wonderfully tasty fruits to be enjoyed by all. She knows how to care for delicate orchid flowers hanging high above the ground in the splendid rain forests. Do you think her supreme intelligence cannot, therefore, lead you on the spiritual path according to your unique nature?

She has appointed different spiritual teachers to do her work. How can you expect the spiritual teacher to teach everyone in the same way?

Your future is not the same as Raja's. He may want to become a sannyāsin. You may like to marry. He may be a very intelligent boy who picks up my teachings in an instant. Another person may be a little slow. Raja is an Indian boy – you are from a western country. How can you pin down the guru to behave the same with everyone?

So the first step to having faith is just simply to believe in your guru. If I, Swamiji, say that I will solve a problem, don't think, "Oh, will he do it and can he do it? Shall I ask him again?" If I say something will happen, it definitely will, but I won't tell you when. Patience is part of your teaching programme. I will solve your problem, but you must also mature while I do so, don't you think?

Next, you asked me how you can stop worrying. Well, if you are determined to remain engrossed in your ego-self, always thinking in a selfish way, then surely you cannot stop worrying. If you are worried, then you are being selfish about something. You think only your problem is big and so your amount of worry is just as big.

You worry so much because you think only of yourself and not of others or their problems. How to stop worrying? Surrender all that is in your mind to God. God will make you happy, solve all your mental problems and cure physical diseases.

If you are always criticizing, it means you have the mind of a monkey. Not only that, you have a very narrow mentality. When you criticize others too much, the first step to stop this awful habit is to laugh. Laugh at yourself and then ask yourself truthfully why you are feeling bad about others and what they are doing. Ask yourself repeatedly, "Why, why, why?" The true answer will come into your mind automatically.

Do not be angry with yourself when you enquire into your mind. When you research your own faults, you should be kind with yourself. Relax and be still. Reduce tension and excitement. Ask with kindness and love. Talk to your own mind in a friendly way and question it slowly and carefully.

Everyone likes love. If you are always angry, your mind will not listen to you. You must talk with love. You expect everyone else's love and so why do you not expect your own? Do you think that your love is cheap and has no value? The problem is that you do not understand the value of the divine love that is inside you. That is why I have come to show you the wealth of pure love that is hidden deep within you.

Yes, sometimes I must be a little hard with you to make you realize your faults. In this way, I will take you quickly on the spiritual path.

All my actions are full of divine love. I do everything for your own good. Take this opportunity at once and practise what I tell you, today itself!

# Do you know how to listen?

Tamil is a great language. It is the most ancient in the world. It is so expressive that it is difficult to truly translate its vast vocabulary which is full of deep feeling and rich, spiritual meaning. In Tamil, we say that sevi jnānam is the wisdom of listening.

Many people talk, but few know how to truly listen. If you listen carefully to good advice, you can correct yourself and gain spiritually. Listening correctly is the first step in a chain of spiritual reaction. After listening carefully, you will start to observe more outwardly and inwardly. Thereafter, you will benefit from analyzing your inner feelings. We realize much once we start to honestly examine our inner feelings.

The greatest sevi jnānam is when we are in the company of highly evolved souls. They are doing work that is far beyond the ability of the ordinary human being. Whatever they say or think will happen. Ordinary people have no idea what great souls are truly doing in this world. If you are lucky to be in the presence of a saint when he or she is giving satsang, you are greatly blessed. There is a special energy in their words. Along with their exceptional knowledge, divine vibrations will be absorbed into your body.

True transference of wisdom from the saint does not just come to you because he is paying lip-service to the ideals of spirituality or talking very well on a spiritual subject. A genuine saint can spark the inner flame within you by his own 'electric' force. The divine spark of knowledge will jump from his heart to yours. His is a fully-fledged fire of wisdom, and its flames bring forth an extraordinarily powerful energy through the mouth of the saint. That energy comes to you through your ears. However, you also listen in a special way – through your spiritual centres. This is sevi jnānam.

Wisdom is like electricity. Normally, we cannot see electricity as a tangible thing without wires and light bulbs. One may feel the spiritual vibration, however. No one can see electricity, but if it touches you it can knock you out or even kill you! This is the secret power of electricity. Spiritual power is infinitely greater than mere electricity. Spiritual power guides and rules the entire universe.

The saint is transferring spiritual energy to you so that you may feel and understand a little of the reality of God. In order to see this you need some light. Thus, the saint's inner light is much brighter than yours so that he can light up your way on the spiritual path. He lets you see where you are going and what obstacles you will meet. Then he shows you how to get over them. When you see a holy person, you must immediately feel that God is within him or her and in that way you will gain divine grace.

The radiant light in the enlightened person is called jagadjyoti. This means the universal light. This radiant light is in everyone but it is very apparent in spiritual people. Your jagadjyoti is not yet visible because you have not cleaned the layers of dirt off the light bulb that is your soul. That's why the pure light cannot yet shine through you. Clean and purify yourself to let this lovely light shine.

This is why I urge you to attend satsang, hear good things and listen to the words of the wise. It is a great opportunity in life to do so. Realize the value of all that is spiritual.

Above all, you have a responsibility towards your fellow beings not to hurt their feelings through your own words. Try not to allow them to hear wrong or hurtful words from your mouth.

Human life is like a puzzle. It is best to always think before you act. Think before you speak. It is not nice to just say what you like to others. It is indeed a spiritual sādhana never to speak in anger but always with love. Please try this from today; you will make yourself and this world much happier.

# Starting in meditation

What is spirituality? Spirituality is a very wonderful and great subject. Throughout the world and through the ages, much has been written and said in a traditional way about spirituality. We do not need money to study spirituality. It is not necessary to think about the colour of one's skin, one's race or religion. We do not need to think of the differences between the people of the East or West. This is a subject for everyone, regardless of who they are or where they come from.

It is normal that when a child reaches adolescence, the mind starts running here and there. At that time it would be best to control the mind but what actually happens is that at this time he or she starts to follow thoughts without discrimination and act according to them. Some people completely give in to the desires of the mind, and they thoroughly spoil and contaminate it. They did not mature their minds in a true sense at all during their teenage years.

However, after becoming adults, many people start to think about what they have done in the past, and they want to realize the Self and lead a proper and correct life. Some people already live a truthful and honest life and, at a later stage, it dawns on them that they also want to live in a spiritual way.

I am from the East, and I follow eastern culture, but the spirituality I teach is universal. However, spiritual training involves culture also, and so the two cannot really be separated. You have to follow spirituality according to the culture of your spiritual master and his environment.

If you follow spiritual life in the Indian way and you are in India, you need to follow the Indian culture. Similarly, if you start your spiritual life in the West and you live there, you also have to live according to the western culture. Despite this, the basic practices of spirituality never change. Likewise, wherever you are, meditation practices never change.

In order to practise true meditation correctly, you need direct contact with a guru or master. Before starting meditation, everyone should get the blessings of the guru. One can get the blessings from the guru's disciples also.

What are blessings? The guru possesses an extraordinary vibration. That spiritual vibration can be transmitted at will by the guru to another, and it will then work in that person's body or mind. Sometimes the guru gives a lingam or statue or some other object containing a strong spiritual vibration to his disciples. That too can transmit an extraordinary spiritual vibration. These are two forms of blessings.

Some devotees do not realize the power of the things I have given to them because they still live in māyā, worldly illusion. To get out of māyā meditation is necessary. If you live with a divine person, no karma, the results of your past deeds, will touch you but māyā will affect you. To get away from māyā and to learn how to control yourself, you need meditation.

Meditation can be likened to burning an oil lamp. First you have to put a wick in the lamp and then pour in the oil. The burned wick should be regularly cut off and then only will it burn properly and brightly. Likewise, we light the wick of spirituality in our hearts. To do this it is necessary to pour the oil of divine grace through the mind and purify it.

Unnecessary thoughts will form, like the dark, burned end of the wick. For our meditation to flourish and shine, the dark part of the wick (the tainted, impure thoughts) must be cut away. Then only will our meditation be effective and it will enlighten us. We have to watch carefully that the flame of the oil lamp does not blow out because of the wind and we should take care that it does not run short of oil. Likewise, let's pray for divine grace to engulf us and clean our hearts and minds. We should not allow the winds of māyā to blow out our bright light of meditation.

Make yourself ready to meditate. Those who are truly interested should do it daily, without stopping, for at least six months at a stretch. They will certainly then realize the benefit. If you wish, I will guide you. You only have to ask sincerely.

# Spiritual powers

I am surprised at the number of people I meet who want to have spiritual powers. These powers are also known as siddhis. In truth, this kind of desire is not conducive to spiritual development.

I never asked to get healing powers or the power to materialize things. This divine gift was with me since I was a very small child. It was there without my conscious knowledge. Whatever I thought of happened and whatever I wished for appeared in my hands. Very soon, people came to know this and, because of these powers, they wanted to be around me. So I had to learn to control this gift very quickly. I only use it if Divinity allows it and I only perform miracles for spiritual reasons and for those who are genuine. These miracles are not my personal wish – I have no personal wish. My life is dedicated to God.

That is why I will never say that anyone can learn to perform miracles. I materialize religious and spiritual objects for worship or vibhūti for healing. This is not magic, nor is it to show off my power. This is done to help the sick and dying and to guide spiritual aspirants on the path. Lingams materialize from my body for these same reasons and they are used for the benefit of humanity. My powers are not for sale. I never ask money for any miracles. That is entirely wrong. To ask money for healing by any of my materialized objects is also very wrong and I have never sanctioned this kind of 'spiritual sale.'

Spirituality is common property. It is the birthright of every creature in the universe. It is not for sale. It is the purest 'commodity' available for human beings and it has the greatest value on earth.

Only those who are spiritually mature should heal others or perform miracles. In order to become spiritually mature, there are many stages and levels of all kinds to experience, understand and realize. Severe tests must be undergone again and again. If you tell me you want to become spiritually mature, I may ask you why. If you say you want spiritual power, that is an immature answer. The correct answer is that you want peace of mind or you want perfect happiness. These are sincere answers.

Do not think that because you had one or two psychic experiences here and there that you are ready, to guide others on the path. If you are not ready, they will fall down and you will also fall. Only your guru knows when you are ready to help others and, at that point, he will instruct and guide you exactly how to do it. You should follow his every instruction to the letter and then you will be sure that you are really helping others.

The best thing you can do is to direct people straight to your master. That is the greatest gift you can give to them. You should not be selfish about this. They could go straight to him...why should they go through you? Do not try so fast to teach others yourself. It is not going to help you in the long run.

I advise you not to announce your healing abilities or psychic and spiritual experiences to others. If you tell everyone you will not benefit. It is better to keep quiet. There is time for everything. When God wants you to heal others or help them in a spiritual way, you will definitely and surely be informed by your spiritual master.

Until that time, wait patiently, practise meditation and worship sincerely. Give selfless service to others as your master tells you. All will happen according to God's wish.

# Tasting divine nectar

Your body is made up of substances which were originally produced inside your mother's womb. Even animals are produced in the same manner. When the foetus needs nutrients, it takes them through the placenta from the blood of the mother. When the foetus is born, what is it looking for? It always expects some form of nutrition. When your body has lost nutrition, it gets tired. The body always demands what it has been used to according to its habit, even before it was born. Everyone has some form of parasite in the body. When the parasites do not get sufficient food for themselves, the body reacts and becomes tired.

If you want to practise the spiritual life, first you must give your body sufficient nutrition to stop it from getting exhausted. There is no harm in reducing excess food. You may even reduce your liquid intake. However, there are certain nutrients that are essential for the maintenance of the body. Just because you are living a spiritual life and you hope to see God and achieve a high stage, it does not mean that you should allow the body to deteriorate physically. On the other hand, you should not waste 24 hours a day for the upkeep of the body. You should give the body only what is necessary. But do keep in mind that you need the body to achieve a high spiritual state.

You need a piece of paper to make a drawing. You need a block of stone to produce a sculpture. You need many materials to build a house. Likewise, to find out the truth, your body is essential. If you feel faint, giddy or exhausted, then the body has lost resistance. At such times you should give it the necessary vitamins and nutrition.

When a very high state has been achieved then a certain form of nectar (amritam) is formed on the tongue. That nectar goes into the body and maintains it. When such a stage is achieved during meditation, or when it occurs naturally as part of steady spiritual progress, you may come to the point where the body does not need worldly food. One may reach this stage and receive divine nectar naturally, but one may still also take food. This stage can only be reached by one who is submissive and very humble, who cultivates pure good habits, quietness and stillness of mind, the purest and deepest love and excellent good qualities. Such a great state can certainly never be achieved by someone who spends their entire time gossiping rubbish and allowing the mind to run from one thing to another like a jumping monkey.

When you think you know everything you can never achieve anything. Nectar forms in the mouth of one who is well on the road to enlightenment. When you come close to this stage, the amritam gives you the strength to achieve enlightenment. Until that point you should not assume that you have approached this stage.

These things all happen naturally after long periods of spiritual training under a true teacher. However, digging the well is your job and water will only ooze out when you reach the water table. What is important is whether there is actually a spring of water where you are digging the well. You must work hard to reach the water. If your teacher is genuine and you are sincere, the spring will be there, and you will reach it.

Be patient and have devotion. When you constantly practise patience and devotion, you will reach the stage of formation of amritam. This will then give you the extra divya shakti (divine force) to attain enlightenment. Until you reach that stage, you will have to maintain your body well.

I pray that you will all taste Divinity!

# Facing problems

I n the ancient days the guru expected his disciples to have implicit faith in him and that even if he told them to jump into a well, they would do so. Even that is not so difficult a test if you know that the guru takes full responsibility and that he has the power to save you from death.

However, in this modern age, a far more sophisticated and understanding state of mind is expected on the part of the disciples and devotees. They need to develop a maturity in facing the tricky, cunning and low moral values of the world today. To jump in the well required blind faith. What I am stressing is the kind of mental maturity that brings about equanimity of mind. Whatever the outcome of any situation, one should develop the state of mind to accept all eventualities without being shaken up or disturbed.

Success should not elate you, nor failure frustrate you.

When I accept someone as a devotee or disciple, I take full responsibility for their spiritual guidance and also their karmas (results of past deeds which they must experience). I test them without many of them realizing what I am doing. You see, it is useless to teach spiritual ideas all the time. People tend to learn them and then forget them. They may have learned certain values by heart but they carry on their day-to-day lives in the same old way.

I prefer to make my students learn by practical spirituality. This way is a little tough, but it has a great and lasting effect. There is nothing new to teach in spirituality. All that has to be learnt has already been said by others. Why should I continue to add and add to their wisdom?

My way is to constantly prompt my disciples and devotees to face problems and provocations, difficulties and irritations so that they automatically learn by themselves. If they have a deep sense of commitment towards Divinity, they are guided along the correct path naturally. If they do not learn they have to face the same test again.

It is not necessarily I who gives such tests and problems. It is Divinity itself. The fact that one has come into the orbit of my influence means that one has to face problems. How many are able to face up to these tests? Those who face up to challenges with humility and determination find themselves automatically progressing quickly on the spiritual path. Think of difficulties as blessings that make you stronger and stronger.

Don't think that anyone gets left behind just because they seem to be shaken by life and its many lessons. They too are slowly learning. They too will progress. Also, do not imagine that the spiritual path is always full of pain and suffering. It is also full of joy and light! I have not been affected by all that has happened around me. In fact, my arrest and imprisonment have been great opportunities to be close to people who are usually ignored by society.

# Use your eyes wisely

For spiritual purposes our eyes are very important organs of the body. When you speak with a person you may look directly at them, but some people move their eyes around, looking down or sideways. Our eyes do not have the capacity to cheat or lie. Our eyes are not jealous, deceitful or egotistical. Our eyes are honest organs.

Eyes never allow dirt from outside to enter the body. If dust falls, the eyelids close automatically to protect the eyes. Tears flow to protect the eyes and flush out dirt particles. Likewise, the eyelids can also protect the eyes from allowing external ideas from entering the mind.

Our eyes do not have unwholesome qualities, but the mind does. The mind observes through the eyes and it always comments on what it sees. The mind cannot keep quiet about what it observes. The eyes are simply organs of seeing – it is only the mind that makes all kinds of thoughts. Our eyes are faultless, but the mind spoils them! It is the mind that directs the eyes in the wrong direction. If one takes this point of view, one can see that the body is divine. It is the mind who is the naughty one. It is the connection to the mind that leads you astray.

In all the languages there is a saying that advises us not to believe only that which is seen. In English, you say "All that glitters is not gold."

Eyes can be used wisely to help you in spirituality. They can uplift you if you carefully observe and learn. When you use the eyes with ego, they will take you away from the spiritual path.

On a simple level, when the feeling to sleep comes the eyes close themselves, and they are absorbed in sleep. No force is necessary. It is a natural happening. Then the body is absorbed in sleep for normal rest. At this time the eyes do not allow the mind to register anything from outside and disturb the body. When the eyes are not involved in seeing, the body can take rest. Likewise, we can use our eyes wisely and still the mind for meditation. Through self-training one can instruct the eyes to see but not allow the mind to react to what is seen. Just as one sleeps, put the mind to rest and make it peaceful.

When you react to what you see you may get irritated and angry. You feel stress and get tension throughout the body. You might get palpitations and high blood-pressure. These tensions in the mind reduce your sattvic (calm and pure) qualities. When you have such reactions and tendencies, they are of no benefit to you whatsoever. Such reactions are only destructive. They drag you down and pull you away from your spiritual path. Seeing and becoming involved in what is seen creates such unwanted problems.

Looking at others with dislike, hatred or anger, wounds the minds of others and reduces your own purity of mind. There is truth in the old cultural beliefs of the evil eye. Try not to look at others with jealousy, dislike or any kind of ill-feeling. You can hurt them.

One must not be attached to what is seen. Be as if you are a blind person to outside activities that are not worthwhile. Tell your mind not to get involved with unwanted and unnecessary things just because the eyes have seen them. Use your eyes with discrimination.

You know that it is God who gave us these wonderful eyes but you always use them to look at others, and you allow the mind to comment, "Oh! she is beautiful, she is fat, he is ugly, he is dirty" and so on. Really, what should you look at? You should look very closely and critically at yourself. Your eyes always see others when you should look at yourself. I do not mean that you should look in a mirror. That is a reflection of the body, of māyā. Whether your physical eyes are open or closed, think about yourself.

Instead of observing what everyone else is doing, start to think...how long are you going to stay in the Ashram, what sādhana are you going to do in this life, what teaching have you absorbed? It is better to examine yourself by thinking, "Was I a help or a nuisance to others today? Did I go astray and do anything wrong? Did I wound the hearts of others with my sharp tongue?" See inside yourself and think carefully.

Do you think it is only wrong if others hurt you? Is it not wrong if you hurt them? Look mindfully and deeply into your consciousness. Did you act in a spiteful way or with the idea of revenge? Revenge is the way of the cruel mind.

In spirituality, one who is leading and correcting others should be one whose mind is always in equanimity. Shānti (peace) is not just a word to be repeated thoughtlessly at the end of your prayers. It is a sacred mantra, a word of divine power. It is a most important feature of the spiritual life.

Your mind needs to become peaceful in order to progress.

When one is truly happy the eyes will shine. On a genuinely smiling, joyful face the eyes join in and smile sweetly. When you really, truly experience real happiness from pure devotion you will shed tears of sheer joy. Sorrowful tears arise from sadness. Even if a person of steady mind gets upset, the eyes show it. In Tamil, we say, "Agattin allaku mugattil teriyum." This means that one can see the beauty of the inner nature in the face. I simply say that if one sees the eyes as the focal point of the face, that is enough.

Divine Mother has given us eyes as a wonderful gift but so many of you cannot truly see.

Pray that she gives you the grace to use these eyes correctly to help you on your spiritual journey. May her light make your eyes shine always.

# The nature of desire and how to overcome it

Everyone born as a human being has desire. Every being created by God has desire. When desire overpowers you, it makes you dance to the tune of your feelings and emotions.

Desire has very many forms. One of them is greed, another is selfishness. Greed is a desire that makes you want more wealth, more property, more jewellery and so on. However, all people who acquire various kinds of wealth and material belongings should not be described as greedy. In day-to-day life certain things are essential, and we consider them as necessary items for our living. Everything we acquire that is really necessary for us in our daily life should be considered as essentials and not as greed. At the same time, when we acquire more material things than are really necessary, that which cannot be called essential, that is one form of greed. We keep on thinking, "This is for me, for me, for me" and we continue collecting things. Another form of desire is vanity. You always want to beautify the body with clothes and make-up. Yet another form of desire is to always want to appear superior to others. This type of desire arises without our being very much aware of it.

Desires are caused by allowing the monkey mind to wander uncontrollably. It wants so many things. It wants a good name and a special position in life. Because of these aims, desires take control of you. You then always try to get more and more wealth, you want to be more well-known, and you want to boost your ego in other ways.

Yet another form of desire is to make others think that you have achieved a high spiritual state. Some people boast that they have seen God when they really have not had such an experience. Such a person wants to impress others that he is a great spiritual devotee.

Considering all these desires, how can you discover what is genuine in yourself? Think carefully. Do you want to get more and more property? Why? Are you not secure with just one place to live in? Do you fear for your children's future? Do you worry about what others think of your home? All this is māyā, illusion. It will not help you on the spiritual path. You can take nothing with you when you leave this earth except the grace you acquired during your lifetime.

Do you love money? Do you want much more than is necessary for you to live? Why are you so attached to your money? Live simply and healthily and try to do some service to the poor and genuinely needy with some of your extra money. If you regularly give a little money away for a good cause, you will feel less attached to your money. Some people find it difficult to give even a small amount because they are so attached to their wealth, and they have become totally selfish and suspicious of those who try to do good in the world. Their absolute attachment and desire for money make them like this. Others, who hardly have any money at all, graciously give more than they can afford to the very poor or to help spiritual institutions.

Look at yourself. Are you a mean or a generous person? Are you very attached to a few rupees? Can you take all your money with you when you die? Certainly not. Think about your feelings regarding money and carefully consider them. Be honest with yourself.

Another form of desire is for a loving relationship. A man and woman's affection for each other is natural but it is still a bodily desire. It is said that there is no end to these kinds of desires. Many people do not believe that a human being can live happily without a partner or without sex. However, this is not so. One can live very happily without these desires, and such a life can encourage personal growth, peace and contentment. The majority are not prepared to accept that this is true. Why? Because they have so much sexual desire and it is controlling them. They cannot control their desire, and so they refuse to believe that others can live without sex.

Desires are difficult to continually fulfil, and desire tends to generate more desire. At some stage you need to say, "Enough – I have had enough!" Then you will see through the true nature of desire. Refuse to become its slave. Be a master of your desires. Don't let the desires master you! At some stage you will feel mental satisfaction that what you have, or have experienced, is enough.

Pride is a dangerous and harmful quality. Being proud of yourself, plus the desire to be superior over all others is a total delusion. In the extreme, such a superiority complex could delude you into believing you are greater than even the supreme Lord Shiva. There are stories demonstrating this kind of behaviour in the Hindu scriptures.

Some people feel that the spiritual master is their own personal property. They think that he must teach only them, he must be only with them, he should not talk to others, he must laugh only with them, he should not instruct others in dharma, only them, and that they are everything to him. This is certainly not the right approach. This way is full of wrong desires. True, it is best to have devotion to your spiritual teacher, but you must also know how to behave with him or her. You should not allow your thoughts to overpower you and feel that he must teach only you. You should be humble and obedient to your spiritual guide, and you must understand and know how to respect him.

The genuine guru is the embodiment of supreme grace. The supreme grace of God is the same as the grace of the guru. The guru has come to teach you higher spiritual knowledge. The guru is the person who has come to teach you how to love God. The guru has come to educate you in Divinity. It is the guru who has come to guide you to the truth. Therefore it is best not to have any selfish thoughts regarding the guru. When selfish pride overtakes you, you might believe that the guru only belongs to you. People mostly approach spiritual masters with a certain amount of worldly desire. They mostly ask him to satisfy their worldly desires. Only a few genuine people come to ask to develop their ātma. This desire is a worthwhile one. I am happy to see those who have this great desire.

There is a way to get rid of desire. How? The day that you decide to overpower desire, do not give first place to it. Take control of your thoughts and ensure that they do not overpower you. You can start checking and directing your thoughts and pray to the divine power to help you concentrate your thoughts on the highest. Try to associate with good people. Ask God to bless you so that your mind always dwells on the Divine, "In this world, oh God, whatever anyone does to me, give me the strength not to care or worry about it. Even if desire tries to overcome me and make me its slave, let God's grace stop me from dancing to desire's tune!"

So, how can you practically get over desire? Make a firm decision. Thoughts are like monkeys, and they jump from branch to branch of the tree that is our mind. Take control of the monkeys and stop them running everywhere! This is where you need the grace of God and the grace of the spiritual master to build up your will-power and achieve one-pointed concentration in the mind.

How can you do this? Keep on repeating only good things to the mind. Tell it not to be in a hurry but to be patient and think of God. Ask it to think carefully before carrying out any action and question what will be the consequences. Is what you are going to do helpful to you on your spiritual path? Will it increase or decrease your attachments?

Control your thoughts with love. Don't rush. Be steady. You cannot attain self-control overnight. It takes time.

Lead your mind slowly and carefully onto the correct path. Ultimately, the surest way to control desire is to bring yourself closer and closer to the Divine. Then desire automatically and steadily falls away from you. There is no need to force yourself. Call for me, and I will help you.

# How fast can you learn spirituality?

Why are you always in such a hurry to get through life? You want to do so many things and experience everything you possibly can in life, so fast. This is the modern life. There are lots of complex electronic gadgets available to perform all kinds of work. Computers make work go faster and faster. If the machine is slow people get tense and upset. At the touch of a button, you can do hundreds of detailed jobs in seconds. This is the latest technology, and it is suitable for the modern world, but the spiritual way is entirely different. In fact, it is the opposite. In the spiritual life, the aim is to make the mind still and peaceful.

Do you think that you can learn from spiritual masters at such a speed and within a certain time limit? Are you thinking in terms of days, weeks, months or years? In reality, there is no set time to learn spirituality. How you learn and how quickly depends on a number of factors.

How interested are you in spirituality? Spirituality cannot be understood just by taking a one-month course. Spirituality pervades your whole lifestyle, and you need to be constantly aware of it and realize that you will have to practise it your entire life. Those who are fully absorbed in spiritual life and who truly want to reach the highest divine state, wish to be aware at every moment.

First, you must understand the point of spirituality. Many people think they know a lot about spirituality, yet they truly do not understand its bare essentials. It is to elevate us to our highest peak of evolution and make us perfect. It enables us to understand the Self and realize that Self. It exists to show us that there is a great force beyond all in existence. It is there to release us from unawareness and to make us understand that we came into existence because of that great force. Spirituality gives us understanding so that we can discriminate between what is good and what is bad. It helps us look deep inside and know ourselves. Above all, it helps us achieve inner freedom.

Think of how much interest you have and how much of your life you are willing to dedicate to spirituality. How fast you progress depends on your earnestness, how sincere you are and how much effort you are willing to put in. These are the determining factors in how quickly you will progress. When you try to go close to God, God will help you by coming closer to you in some way.

If you are gifted to come into contact with a true spiritual teacher who can guide you correctly, you must understand that it is in this way that God has taken many steps towards you and is leading you towards him through the teacher. God comes down from his supreme position of the highest level of existence. Therefore, surely it is not much to ask that you reach out as much as you can and do all that is necessary to come close to him, is it?

You see, people can learn book knowledge by reading, but that is not practical experience. They can read Vedānta philosophy, for example, in one week and they can study the many other aspects of Sanātana Dharma in a few more weeks. You might read the teachings of Lord Buddha in a day, but you can never practically attain in 24 hours the mighty state that Lord Buddha reached! After a long time of soul-searching, renunciation and asceticism, he sat in the jungle in one place for seven long years in order to attain inner freedom.

You may be able to quote freely from all the scriptures in the world but does this mean that you have genuine experience of God? Some of the greatest saints in the world from many different religions, were (and are) illiterate or from the poorest of backgrounds. Their pure hearts and free minds, full of divine love, allowed God to make them glorious examples to humanity.

You should consider what you really want to learn and how genuine you are in your aspiration. One who is really straightforward and honest will progress quickly. Some want to attain liberation; some people think they should get divine energy for some purpose or another. Some want to get spiritual knowledge fast because they want to be in the position of spiritual master over other aspirants and some want to show the public that they know everything – they want to display that they are superior to others. Some want to learn something fast so that they can charge others and get money for their 'spiritual services' and 'blessings'. Those who have ulterior motives will not grow quickly. They must first clean out their minds and severely reduce the ego. What are your true feelings?

You sometimes wait for me for one, two, three or even eight hours to come and talk to you and give satsang. You feel impatient and uncomfortable. You notice all your bodily aches and pains, how hot it is or how hungry you are. There are so many things you want to do and so many unnecessary thoughts flashing through your minds whilst you are waiting for me. You are all in a hurry, but I want something else for you. I want you to become genuinely spiritual, and so I make you wait. It is a test that is very good for your training in patience and also your concentration on the Divine.

To be successful on the spiritual path, it is essential to develop patience and humility. Be hungry for knowledge of God. You are all in such a hurry. Be patient and do your best to think of the Divine as much as you can. Why are you in a hurry? You cannot win the great prize of divine knowledge in a short time. Firstly, you must practise. Secondly, you must purify your mind, and thirdly you must get peace in your heart. Then only will you understand the true value and meaning of spirituality.

May you all experience the great stillness within. My love and blessings are yours.

Be still for some moments and know that I am with you.

# Spirituality, marriage and children

The greatest teaching is by example. Look first at your home life. What is the meaning of married life? Essentially, you live together and have sex so that you can have children.

Marriage today often means divorce tomorrow. Many people get divorced very quickly, but I take the traditional view that marriage should be a lifelong commitment to one partner. You should be together for your entire life, no matter what difficulties come your way. That is the real meaning of marriage. You need to be tolerant, practical, patient and forgiving. If you have a car and some parts go wrong, as it gets a little old you will throw it out and change it. You cannot treat a human being like that! Will you just use the body and mind of your partner and when something goes a little wrong you say, "Get out!"? This is not right according to our ancient culture. Marriage is for life, for better or for worse. This is the way you need to teach your children otherwise they will never understand the value of marriage and family life. Teach them now, early in life, otherwise later on when things go wrong, you will have so much worry.

It is good to show your children the love that you say is in your heart for them. Show them so much love that the child really feels your love. When you die, that child must really feel it very deeply that you are gone.

The child too needs to revere and respect the parents. Imagine how children feel when their parents split up. If the father goes off with another woman and the child sees his mother in mental agony and always in tears, do you think he will have a strong love for the father? He is more likely to start hating him. He will feel completely fed up with his parents.

Children feel family disturbances and upsets very much. They touch them very deeply. You put this unstable mentality into their minds when they are young and later they will do the same thing themselves because you have spoiled their minds. Try not to show the wrong way to them. Do your best not to fight in front of the children. Wait until they have gone to school! Do not teach them to be angry and fight all the time. When they are out of the house you can have a nice big argument and throw and break things, but not in front of the children!

The future of this world lies in the hands of your children. If you want to eat good food, first you need natural, good quality seeds and to make sure that the seeds have not spoiled or gone bad. Then you will harvest good crops and feed many people. The natural and most valuable seeds of this world are the children. You need these living seeds for this world to reach a high spiritual state. So don't spoil the seeds. Look after them very carefully. If you raise these good seeds very well, they will take care of the spirituality on earth after our deaths. They will be in charge of spirituality on this planet in years to come. But right now, the poor examples of many parents, the excessively materialistic and sensual environment and the media are spoiling our good seeds.

I plan to grow many good seeds. I will look after them very carefully and teach them. I will take young seeds that others do not want. I will take you also, even though you are late and somewhat old seeds!

Some children are depressed or narrow-minded, some have ego, some are jealous, some are a little mad, and some are very naughty. When I see the many hundreds of children who are being brought up in the Ashram, I can see all the different mentalities that are in this world. Some have no mother or father, and some have only one parent who cannot afford to raise them, or they have some other family problems. Even if you raise problem children with very much love, often they cannot understand this love. So, in such cases, how can we turn them into good seeds? It is very necessary to have endless patience with them. First, you must show them love, and after that you must be very, very patient. You have to be willing to repeat their lessons time and time again.

Of course, children have faults, and they make many mistakes. But they are only children! They are pure-hearted and have soft, pliable minds that can be corrected.

141

If you show love to them and teach them, they will work hard and learn the correct ways in life. Talk kindly with them and explain. Sometimes discipline is necessary. You will suffer if you allow your children to rule you.

Another very essential thing to bring up children well is to allow yourself time to be with them. You allow yourself time to sleep, to cook, to eat, to talk to friends on the telephone, to go to work, to enjoy yourself. You should see to it that you also allocate time every day to talk to your children.

Firstly, husband and wife should take time to sit together and talk for at least an hour every day. Only sit and talk. Do not have physical contact at this time as this creates a different kind of attachment. Talk slowly and carefully about your problems.

Then call your children one by one. If you have more than one child, it is not always useful for the children to speak to them together. First, call one child and chat for some time, then the other one. Talk very nicely and kindly and with lots of love. Ask them their difficulties. Ask them to be honest with you and try to help them with everything. Explain to your child that he or she must grow up in a good way and give them nice advice. If you do this regularly, the children are not as likely to get into problems. You will get good seeds.

All parents should understand the technique of talking nicely and in depth to each other. Firstly, mother and father must understand the value of each other and then they can fully realize the worth of their raising lovely children.

Do not forget, it is a big sādhana to bring up children spiritually. Give them good ideas and teach them about faith, trust and confidence in God.

# Parents must teach children spiritual values

The most important thing to ensure that children learn spiritual values and gain higher understanding is that the parents have a spiritual mentality. Even so, they might explain much to their children, but the children may find it difficult to grasp spiritual values. Why? Because of the modern culture, environment and way of living that are not at all favourable to learn spiritual values.

The minds of the children are going in the opposite direction. They think they must enjoy everything they possibly can in this world and they want many comforts. They think this world will make them happy. This is because of the television, what their friends tell them, what the newspapers and magazines say and what they see in their daily lives.

Yet I can only say that it is the parents' essential duty to give the children faith and trust in the Divine. If you help your child to develop spiritually, that is one thousand times better than teaching him or her anything else. Of course, children must do their normal routine studies, but, these days, schools are not like they used to be. They do not generally teach moral values and religion, and so we must do these things at home.

You developed in your own way later in life, and you took the decision on your own to follow a spiritual path. How wonderful would it have been if you had been given this opportunity when you were young! As it was, in most cases, nobody taught you in your youth. Now you are interested in the divine way. However, you are educated people and have some knowledge about the world. You are not innocent children who know nothing about life and neither are you fools. You know what is true and what is false. You understand what is bad and good. You can judge many matters for yourself with discrimination, and you will not go on the wrong path. As intelligent, educated people, therefore, I can assume that you are going in the right direction in life.

So, how can you take your children in the right direction? You need to take a great deal of time and, very lovingly, turn the children on to the correct path. You could say that maybe it is better to leave them to make their own decisions and experience and discover spirituality on their own. But my advice is that when that time comes, it could be very late. At least give them the chance now.

It is essential to explain spiritual matters very kindly and lovingly to children. These days, some parents are not even in the house for the children when they come home from school. When the children return home, mother is out. Some parents do not give their children enough time. It is really good to take an hour a day to talk to the children with love and interest.

Do you think Indian schools teach religion and values to the children? No. It is their parents who bring them up in a spiritual environment. Indian parents are very good. They are very kind. They take the time to explain spiritual things to children. They do this at home. They go out as a family to spiritual places. They celebrate many spiritual and cultural festivals at home and teach the children how to do rituals and what their deep meaning for the good of their lives is.

Unfortunately, I have seen that some parents even prefer their pet dogs and cats to the children. They allow the puppy and the cat to sleep on their beds, but they don't allow that closeness to their little children. They talk to the dog and put the children in front of the television for the evening. What is the meaning of this? Your dog understands your love, and he shows it by wagging his backside, but the children don't understand. They only know the television programmes, many of which make them into dependent, thoughtless beings. So if you want your children to pick up spirituality, you are wasting your time if you do not show them love.

In Hinduism, the one who teaches the dharma, the spiritual codes of life, is called the guru. So before you study seriously under the guru, you meet many assistant gurus. Don't think that a guru is always someone who is a sannyāsin who has renounced the world, or a very

145

highly elevated soul. You are the gurus to your children. You are teaching dharma to them.

It is first of all your responsibility and then, later, maybe mine.

# Swamiji, what do you expect from us?

*Swamiji, sometimes you are very honest and to the point when you indicate our faults. Surely the spiritual master should always teach lovingly?*

I always have love in my heart when I speak to you. You think that someone should speak to you with love just to please you. It depends on the person or the situation. Sometimes it is necessary to be very direct and then only will the aspirant realize his or her mistakes.

Do not expect that the spiritual master has come to please you. He cannot spend his time inflating your ego. Remember, he has come to destroy your ego. On the spiritual path, you cannot expect that the guru will praise you all the time and tell you how well you are progressing. If you are really going ahead quickly on the path, he is more likely to be harder with you to spur you on and test you. Then only you will improve more and more. So, remember, I will not give you cake, butter and jam – but I will lead you to ānandam, permanent and ever-lasting happiness.

*Swamiji, what do you expect from us initially on the spiritual path?*

I always ask first that you develop a strong interest. Without a keen concern about your spiritual life you cannot expect to progress much. You need to be very honest with yourself and identify your faults within your own mind. You must be prepared to analyse yourself and be ready to correct your old ways and worldly habits. In order to do this, train your mind to be strong, courageous and confident. It is not easy to change your old tendencies and lifestyle.

After understanding yourself a little, resolve to make yourself happy, but not through the old material way. I mean real, independent happiness. I am talking about the joy of faith, pure love and fearlessness.

I am not expecting money from you. If you wish to give donations that has to be your own personal decision. I do not expect you to have educational qualifications, although many of my devotees are highly educated. Education is not a condition to learn spirituality. However, I do encourage the youngsters to finish their education to the best of their ability. I do not expect that you should strive for position in work or society. This is often only ego-building, and our point is to lessen the ego.

Love is very necessary but love for whom? Initially, you must love yourself. You should be kind with yourself.

If you are not kind with yourself on the spiritual path, you will not feel like carrying on.

*I find it difficult to stay in one place or with one spiritual master. If I go to see many masters is this not good for me?*

This is one of the eternal questions on the spiritual path. So I will repeat my favourite answer because it is a most important point to keep in mind.

Initially, it is good to see other āshrams and masters and observe these places and people. Experience their great blessings and see if their teachings are suitable for you. However, after some time it is important to settle down in one place and with one master in order to grow.

You may have observed the tube bore-wells in the Ashram. They are operated by a hand-pump. When we want to bore down to find water, do you think it is enough if we just go down five or six metres? No, we must take time and go down thirty metres. Then we will surely find water. If we get fed up after digging five metres and go and start another well, eventually we will find that we have started seven or eight wells, but we never discover water. It would have been better to search for the correct place with patience and then bored the well for thirty metres in the first place. Likewise, if you continually stay a few months in this Ashram, a few in another and another few in yet another and so on, you will never reach the Divine during your entire life. By staying in one place, or practising with one master, you can reach a very high level. This is entirely in your hands.

149

These few answers are short, but they contain a lot of material for you to practise. The key is to practise. In practising you will face the everyday problems of spirituality, and it is your experience in overcoming obstacles that makes you strong.

I always talk to you about patience and love. When you have any problems it is always good to remember these noble qualities. They will see you through all difficulties. Then, of course, you need to have faith. Through faith in your master and the Divine, you can do anything in this world.

You have Divinity inside you but you do not know it. Feel God inside! Then everything will be yours. But first you must truly feel, know and realize that God is inside.

I bless you all that you will realize that everything is in you.

# Love all as yourself

The mind always wants to criticize and see the worst side of things. What can you do to stop this? Try to control your mind by continually asking it to be impartial. The mind should be still. Try not to let it think someone is good, someone is bad. What is the use of having friends or enemies? Treat all alike. See all with an equal eye. What is the point in looking for bad qualities in people? Remember, you know nothing about others. You only see the outside, the very surface of their being. You do not know or understand what they really are.

Who are you to judge others? First, clean up your own mind. Look at your own bad qualities and clear them out of you. These tendencies are the naughty people, not those around you. Once you have cleaned up yourself you will never see the weak points in others. They will simply not register in your mind. When a man looks at a woman, he may think that she is his mother, his sister or a prostitute. It all depends on his frame of mind.

Change your mental attitude. Make it open and free, not narrow and criticizing.

Strive to reach a state of mind where you are above all the rubbish in the world. If someone talks nonsense and gossips to you, why do you immediately retain it in your mind? Be like me. I am deaf to all this rubbish. Why do you make your precious mind into a rubbish bucket? What is the point of being gifted with a human birth if you make your consciousness into a garbage heap? Was this the point of your coming to this earth and praying for a spiritual master? Remember, you came here to experience the greatest possible achievement that a human being can attain. Everything around you may be rubbish, but your spiritual duty is to endeavour to be pure in heart.

Vīn pechu in the Tamil language means useless talk. That is a very apt description of gossip. Gossip spoils the mind. It fills it full of untruths. It leads you to think badly of others.

Don't waste your time now. You are growing older every second. Time is passing and death can come at any time. You are in a very good place (the Ashram in India) so make the best use of your stay. There may be a little dirt here and there, but it is useless complaining. Our Ashram is developing slowly. Years ago we had no facilities at all – no water, no toilets, no beds, trees or flowers. The food was very basic. Now you have many conveniences. This spiritual environment is helpful to changing yourself. It inspires good thoughts, actions, right living and charity. Change your mind to always think of these things instead of negative ideas.

Collect all the junk in your mind and put it out into the rubbish pit. Burn it mentally. Then, in the same way, collect all your devotion and store it up in your heart. Always stop the negative tendencies from dirtying your clean and pure devoted heart.

Spirituality is like a golden mango. Its taste is that of divine wisdom. It has a wonderful smell and it is inviting you to taste it. If the fruit that I offer you has a small black spot, will you reject it? No, you will cut it out and eat the fruit. Be like that with everything in life. Don't see the dark spots. Cut them away mentally.

I see only Divinity in people. I am here to help them remove their negative energy and reveal the Divinity that is their true nature. By the way, did you hear that Premananda is in love? I am in love with God! That is why I am truly happy wherever I am. My true love is total. It knows no limits and, what is more, I love you all just like I love God! I have realized true happiness, and because I love you all so much, I want you to realize it also.

That is my wish and blessing for you. I love my Self. You should try to love your Self. Then love all as your Self!

See only the Supreme in everything, everywhere, always.

# The spiritual master smashes the ego

Divinity is without name or form. Discover it. Your spiritual master only wants you to find that. It is not an easy task. That is why the spiritual master comes to you. He has come to guide you and help you because it is difficult.

Guruji tells you that love is God, but you say it seems that sometimes he deliberately disturbs your meditation or ignores you. You ask me why. Guruji is doing this sometimes because if he shows you the extent of his true love, you will become the slave of his love. Remember, his love is very powerful and magnetic. It is like God's love. It is pure, and it is a tremendously powerful, vital and magnetic energy. Everything that guruji does is fuelled by this incredibly dynamic love. The guru loves his devotees intensely, which is why he is filled with kindness towards them and able to repeat the lessons to be learned by them even a thousand times. He initiates the student with extreme kindness and draws the student close. But, thereafter, if he continually allows the student to feel this incredible love, the guru too will be overcome by bliss, and he will be unable to correct and change the student as he wishes.

Guruji wants to remove all the dirt from the minds of those who really desire spirituality. He does this solely so that they can attain a high spiritual state. I want you to have trust, faith and devotion for God. I want you to enjoy bhajans, abhishekams, satsang and meditation. I want you to experience divine thoughts and godly feelings in your heart and throughout your body. I want you to taste ānandam. I want you to have supreme understanding. I want your every action to be divine and have divine meaning.

You came here to me for a divine reason, and so I wish that your purpose in coming should be fulfilled. I want your efforts to bear fruit and so I first help you to dig the soil. I tell you how to plant the little tree of spirituality within you. I explain to you how to ward off the animals that might spoil your baby tree. I even ward them off myself through extraordinary means. I am the gardener tending to you all, my lovely plants. To me, you are all little seedlings in a flower bed. That is how the devotees and disciples incarnate with their sadguru life after life. The connection is as if they were all plants in the same flower bed.

Some people come to me for help with their family problems and diseases. I will cure them. If they tell me their problems and hand them over to me, I will surely help. I only hope that in return they will have more faith in and devotion to God. I feel that God sends you here to me. What do I say to God? I ask God to make this poor world a spiritual place. That is my hope, aim and mission in life. I have no personal desires for anything at all.

People are so narrow-minded in this world. You are all good people, but you have been spoiled by years of living in the materialistic, egocentric world. I want to wash you a little. Washing machines make the clothes clean. The same way the machine works – I will do that same action to you. Watch out, it can be a bumpy ride. When you wear white clothes and go to town, they soon get dirty. After you put them in the machine, they become clean. In the same way, the pure, clean heart that God gave you goes through the world that makes it dirty. I am the washing machine that has come to clean it and make it light and bright. Whatever work God gives me I do very happily. Now he wants me to be a dhobi (Indian washerman).

God has given me many hardships in my life, but I face everything with a smile. There is a purpose for all the hard times he puts me through.

Do not think you have many faults and that I cannot clean you. You have only a few, little wrongs in you. We should never say a person is entirely bad.

So do not misunderstand me too much when I start your intensive training. I do not have to be physically close to you to do this. It happens automatically because you have taken me as your teacher. You get troubles and I may scold you, or you might suffer from a seemingly broken heart for one reason or another. Through all these experiences your ego will be reduced.

If you grow a little spiritually, the ego also grows and creates problems. Finally, the ego will get smashed and then it can never come up again to disturb you. That takes time and much patience.

Always remember that, internally, guruji has infinite love for you but, externally, he cannot show that too much. Once the ego is thrown out the truth will be understood and realized and the ego cannot return. It seems a long and endless process but, believe me, there will be a result for all your striving.

Your guru will then show you how to realize the nameless, formless God.

# The ordinary person and the enlightened soul

Blessed souls, one takes many births before attaining the very rare opportunity of being born as a human being.

Spiritual advancement depends on one's effort and earnestness. After tremendous effort, many tests and painful suffering in the world, one merges with Divinity and becomes one with it. After experiencing the ultimate, matchless happiness and divine light, when the illumined souls see the ordinary, worldly man, they understand that people are unnecessarily entangled in untruth and deceived by illusion. Once all this is realized, the enlightened soul will not become engrossed in worldliness again. That soul will never have the idea of returning to involve itself again in the deceptive, tiresome and temporal life.

One born as a human being becomes a slave to all tests, difficulties and problems. As a result one experiences suffering. Under no circumstances are avatārs (incarnations of the Divine) subject to such suffering. They are always immersed in divine bliss. They are souls matured in God, and they are part of God. They are fully aware that what they experience on earth is the drama of God, or his divine play. Since worldly tests and troubles do not affect them, nor have any effect on them, avatārs do not feel that they are being tested or that they have a problem. Only a person who is immersed in a mundane life considers difficulties as tests or problems.

I have observed that some devotees find it easy to talk or joke about the philosophy of līlās (divine play).Yet if they themselves go through such tests they still suffer tremendously because they have not truly experienced divine understanding.

Throughout the ages and in present times, God has incarnated as a human being and enlightened souls have come to earth with the capacity to experience human feelings, but they are not involved in the illusion of such feelings. This is to develop people and help them to cultivate devotion to God as well as to instil a desire in them to understand the ultimate truth.

Events in the lives of saints happen according to the way of life and the culture prevailing at the time they live in the world. Lord Rama was banished to the forest because of treachery and jealousy. There he helped the forest-dwellers and spiritual aspirants to live purer lives. At the same time, he destroyed the tyrannical rule of the cruel and wicked āsuras, a demonic race that had some extraordinary strength and powers and whose greed and violence was destroying the normal order of life.

Likewise, Lord Krishna, Lord Jesus Christ, Prophet Mohammed, Lord Buddha, Mahatma Gandhi, Sri Aurobindo and many other great souls of Sanātana Dharma and other religions have been tested according to the trends of their times, both social and political.

Nowadays there are people who have no faith in God, but they fool themselves and others pretending that they are great believers who want to do good in the world. Having selfish motives and trying to conceal their own wrongdoings and wicked actions, they attempt to test the saints with wild accusations. They do this according to modern-day trends. They are trying to misuse the law and cheat with scientific technology. They are misleading and cheating the society.

It is good to remember that great souls are not mentally affected by any karma. Karma may appear as good or bad, depending on one's viewpoint and level of understanding. For the enlightened ones, things happen according to the will of God. They know that the Divine will always do what is correct for those who live in truth, whatever the circumstances and outside pressures. Such souls are fearless because they are one with the absolute reality that is all-pervading, all-knowing and all-seeing.

Real faith is beyond all tests, attachment and suffering. An enlightened person is never discouraged or downhearted. Ordinary human beings cannot even imagine such a high state of mind, such endurance, such strength, such joyfulness and, above all, they cannot comprehend the role of the saint in God's drama or plan.

The saint appears to sacrifice himself or herself for the sake of the people. Only later on in the play can you see the plot and the meaning of it all.

The ordinary human being with his jealous and petty ways cannot understand the behaviour of the enlightened person. If he has a personal grudge against the spiritual soul, he may try to pull the saint down to his worldly level by throwing filth and dirt at him. This dirt is the product of his own impure mind and what he has realized from life. However, this worldly dirt cannot stick to the pure saint. His purity and brightness repel the filth yet, for a time, it may seem to ordinary people as if it is there.

Truth will always win.

Society gives an immediate verdict. However, God takes time to give his judgement. You must have the patience to wait for the essential teachings and morals of God's divine drama to be revealed.

May you all come to know the truth.

# The value of the Ashram spiritual activities

Throughout the day in the Ashram there are abhishekams and bhajans. During and after abhishekams there is mantra chanting.

It is traditional in a temple in India to sit down on the ground for these activities. For many foreign devotees, their first sādhana is to learn to sit in the correct manner. At first, your back and legs will hurt you because you are not used to it, but this is a very good training for your future spiritual life and for meditation. Unless, of course, you are getting on in years, try to master sitting correctly on the floor. Slowly increase your time sitting down like this. If you can manage to sit in the half-lotus or full-lotus yoga positions, this is very good.

Sitting through abhishekams and sitting for questions and answers or speeches is really a great yoga. You are keeping still and sitting for quite some time in one place. Your mind is concentrated on spiritual subjects. Watching abhishekams and absorbing their divine energy will help your future meditation immensely. Every religious practice done here is good for your health and the path of spirituality.

When you are singing bhajans, you are singing God's holy names, which bring you closer to your goal of surrendering to your own true Self.

During all the above practices, your thoughts, ideas and brainwaves are all moving in the direction of Divinity. Repeating the names of God purifies the heart and mind. Seated in this way and attending all these sādhana sessions, your body absorbs manifold blessings. All the great saints sang God's name; in doing so, the heart and mind become pure automatically. So during your precious time in the pūjā hall or at your own home shrine, forget all others in the world and pray!

The simplest but most effective mantra chanting, and a great preparation for meditation, is chanting the Aumkaram.

Aum should be said with feeling. It should be chanted somewhat slowly, and the 'M' should be hummed. The breath in between each Aum is very important and time should be given to correctly inhale a long breath. Aum has a great and deep meaning. It is the oldest of all mantras. It is the mūla mantra, the original mantra and it is also repeated as part of other mantras. The sound of Aum embodies the Divine. It is God represented as sound. It will lead you to the ultimate.

The scriptures say that a spider climbs up by means of its web and above it is open space; likewise one who climbs upwards spiritually by meditating on Aum reaches the absolute infinite energy. Aum is everything. It is the past, the present and the future. It can take you to your true Self.

You may feel that after being in the Ashram for a short time, you might not be able to continue such a spiritual life at home. Understand that the spirituality you gain here, and the blessings I give you become part of you and you take them back home with you.

# Light the inner lamp

You are people who have read many philosophical books. This is also a kind of delusion. Certain books, such as the lives of saints, may encourage you on the spiritual path, but studying a lot of complex philosophy at the beginning of your spiritual life will not help you so much. There comes a time when you must say that you have had enough of reading.

Finally, the truths of spirituality are, essentially, oh so simple! When you truly understand something of Divinity, all the knowledge you have accumulated in your head will disappear instantly. Think of books as stepping stones. Don't carry the stones around with you. You will not be able to rise up quickly.

Can you cook a photograph of a potato? No, you must take a real potato and eat it to understand the taste.

Why are you looking at photographs of vegetables but not eating them? The vegetables are there, and you are there...cook and eat! Go deep inside and experience God instead of just reading.

You all talk about higher consciousness, about meditation and about the divine energy. You are all looking and talking. Do something practical. Practise, practise, practise. Only if you do something practical will you get experience. Try not to be just a perpetual student. Go ahead and jump in the ocean of spirituality and try to swim. If you get into difficulties, I will definitely help you if you call out for me.

Remember that knowledge gained from the company of enlightened souls is far superior to any book knowledge. That is why you are extremely lucky and gifted people to meet such souls during your lifetime.

When you start on the spiritual path, the inside of your heart, mind and body is all dark. There is no way light can get in because you are covered so completely with layers and layers of worldliness. God has told me the secret of how to light a small light inside. And so the inside of my heart, mind and body is completely lit up and fully illuminated. Your problem is that you do not know how to ignite this light on your own and so I give you a box of 'spiritual matches' and the correct instructions. I ask you to light the lamp by yourself, but you keep telling me that the flame is continually getting blown out. That is because there is too much wind inside your body. The winds of egoism, desire, jealousy and other such qualities are blowing this way and that way inside you. These things will not allow you to light up the little lamp of spiritual illumination.

If this lamp gets lit and stays burning, these negative qualities cannot do their work. What to do? If you want to light this lamp, you must stop the winds blowing. It is up to you to put in the hard work and follow my advice. You may ask how to stop this wind. Be like small, innocent children. They do not have such winds blowing in them. The winds have not yet started to blow.

Do not think that because you are an adult, you cannot make your mind pure like a child's. I have done it, so why can't you? It is easy and simple to do, but no one likes to do that. Why? Because everyone likes to show that they are superior. They want to pretend that they know everything and that they are powerful people.

Do you want to show off your ego or say that you are a simple person who knows nothing? Those who think they are big might end up being very small and vice versa!

# Inner contact with
# the master

When you meet your spiritual master and you accept, within yourself, that he is your true teacher, you have a major job ahead of you. You have to slowly get rid of your ego, the sense of 'I do' and 'I like' or 'I don't want to.' Surrendering means that one has wiped out the ego and there...you have natural surrender. All your inborn characteristics have to be examined inwardly and slowly removed. Become free and flexible and able to bend with the wind of change, like a simple blade of grass.

A spiritual teacher may be an enlightened soul who has the power to teach thousands of people how to follow spirituality. If he is such a one, he will never show everyone his great spiritual power. He will, most likely, behave like an ordinary person and mix freely with the people he is teaching. This makes it easier for the students to approach him, learn from him and follow his examples.

There is a danger here. Do not fall into the trap of thinking that you know certain things or that you know much more about the world than he does. Just because he does not display his wisdom all the time, it does not mean that you have more knowledge than him. If you feel that he does not know or understand certain matters in spirituality, then you are thinking along the wrong lines. Take the approach that you are a small child and the guru is your spiritual mother or father. He knows what is best for you. The guru does not always want to discuss everything. Your thinking about many subjects and always talking about them is not of value. Try to be simple, humble and patient. This is far better than intellectual gymnastics.

It is not true to think that you will become totally dependent on the guru. Constantly maintaining awareness of the guru as if he is a permanent light in your heart enables you to discover your own inner light. It takes time to develop. It is easier to develop a telepathic contact with your teacher if you are always aware of his presence within you. Through this deep, inner contact, the guru aids the aspirant to reveal the true Self. In this way, by having a strong, personal, direct, inner connection with your spiritual master, he can guide you at every minute in all aspects.

Like a child obeying its mother, you need to learn to accept the advice given to you by the teacher. If you cannot accept simple instructions from your master, how can you go on to higher practices? Learn to follow what the teacher tells you. It is a slow process. Do not try to rush. The teacher will not give you difficult tasks in the beginning.

I have given a simple instruction to many of you who have asked how you can learn from me. At a special time in the morning or evening, take a bath and wear clean, comfortable clothes. Sit quietly in a special place. Think of me for a little while. I will know it and receive your thoughts. I will send blessings and energy to you. Let it work within you. Do this regularly. This is the beginning of sādhana and following the instructions of the teacher. If you do this simple thing, it will help you at all levels of your life. But you have to make an effort.

Getting rid of the ego is the most difficult task on the spiritual path. If you want to become an instrument for the spiritual work to be done on earth and you wish that your teacher should help others by working through you, you must first make the real effort to crush the ego and clean your mind. Then you can train yourself to have the inner contact with your teacher.

This does not happen overnight. It can take years.

# The importance of Brahma muhūrtam

A very important spiritual practice that is essential for everyone on the spiritual path is to get up early, bathe and do some spiritual sādhana. This age-old practice has been carried out in India since time immemorial. The early morning time of four to six a.m. is called Brahma muhūrtam. It is the divinely designated time for all beings to rise and begin their praise of the Divine. Insects, birds, animals and plants start to awaken from their night rest at this time. They all join in one glorious song of praise for God at the dawn of the day.

The ancient sages and rishis, who understood these things from their meditations, told the people to also start the day with praises in this way. During Brahma muhūrtam it is advised not to eat anything because the food will not digest correctly and, therefore, it won't do the body any good.

Getting up early is a great and practical sādhana for every one of my devotees. It is natural, it helps you to develop willpower and, above all, you will be certain to feel God's grace and blessings bestowing many benefits if you follow this practice.

Many of you tell me you have no time for spiritual practices, although you are very interested in doing them. That is why you need to make the effort to get up earlier and do these things. In spiritual life, discipline is very important. By singing devotional songs, chanting ancient prayers, performing meaningful rituals and meditating you can reach a high state. Without actually doing any of these things it is difficult to progress, so why are you neglecting them?

It is important to get up early. I recommend 4 a.m. It is so auspicious and good for you to do this. If you stay in bed late, even until 7 a.m. or 8 a.m., you are doing yourself more harm than good.

There are many valid reasons why you should get up early. You activate the body much better by rising early in unison with everything in nature. Consciously activating the body at this time actually gives you more energy throughout the day. If you get up late, you will feel lethargic and lazy. You will yawn and think of the things to be done in the house, and you won't remember God at all.

Let's not waste one or two hours every single day by sleeping excessively. You think you need so much sleep and that you cannot do without it. Some people are so frightened of not getting at least eight hours sleep per night. They have been conditioned in this way. Can't you give at least one of these hours to God? By dedicating one hour every morning to the Divine, you will certainly reach a higher state of spiritual feeling. That is an extra 365 hours per year for God!

You can always eat and sleep. You can spend your life doing these things. Who gets the chance to think of God? Very few, lucky people. Try to get up early before dawn and bathe. Dress in clean, comfortable clothes and do some spiritual practice. Do what you like best.

Make the effort to try and see how much better you feel. Persevere, and you will certainly attain grace. In this way you will start the day so perfectly and every day will become divine.

What better way to start the day than greeting God himself and praising him? If you do this, your children will also see and understand what you are doing. The best teaching is by example.

# Just be

Summa iru! An often quoted Tamil phrase. It means 'just be.' It applies more to the mind than to the body. It is the greatest spiritual teaching. These two small words encompass so much. Be still and reach inside to your ātma, to your soul. Do not allow the mind to wander here and there.

Let happiness and sorrow come and go – just be. Be balanced and self-controlled. Find out how to always remain happy. Make the mind one-pointed. Do not worry about anything because the Divine is looking after you. You can always do some kind of work with the body but do not think too much about it. Just be.

You will always be successful if the mind is free and calm. Always think that God or guru is with you and you will have a peaceful mind. Turn the mind inwards to the depths of the soul where all is still. This will give you peace.

Drop all thoughts and realize your Self – then all disturbing mind activity will cease. You will know the Infinite. Remain without likes and dislikes and just be.

The true Self is always still but not so the mind. Summa iru, just being, is the secret and mystery of all spiritual practice – yet it is so, so simple. Why do you still want to experience the illusory world? If you simply be still, bliss will overcome you.

When you are totally and truly still, no outside sounds can disturb you. You are busy trying to understand spirituality and to know something. Realize that there is ultimately nothing to learn and nothing to know. You simply have to be totally still.

God is with you all the time, but you do not realize it. Be adaptable and do not agitate your mind. See and understand that the world and everything around you is always changing. We do not do anything. Everything is activated by God, and everything happens according to his will.

Just be, and you will understand all this.

Just be – don't think. Don't think of anything at all. Let thoughts come and go like passing clouds. Just watch them and be their silent witness.

Just be and meditate. To just be is real meditation.

# My first twelve months in prison

I have decided to send this message to you all after receiving requests from many of you that I should write to you personally.

Firstly, I want to assure you all that I am very well. My experience inside the prison is of great benefit to many unfortunate people. Wherever I am, I am immersed in the Divine. During these twelve months away from the world, I was indeed closer to your own loving souls. Always remember that God has given great gifts to me and so I am with you wherever you are and wherever I am.

On a more worldly level, I expect and hope that my being able to manage without a light, without a bed or table and chair and also that I have survived very well on a simple diet, will encourage all of you to reduce your own wants and desires.

1995 appeared to be a difficult time for us all, but I assure you that it will reveal many benefits in times to come. I simply pray to God and allow him to act. I give myself to him. I surrender! I trust and have faith that everything is for the best. How can you know your progress if the Almighty does not test you?

I am delighted with the greatness of my devotees, who, in the darkness of adversity, have demonstrated the power of their constancy and confidence in me. You have indeed passed the test of Divinity. You have discovered the strength of sincerity and truth within yourselves.

In a few days, it will be the New Year, 1996. During the last few weeks, we have shown the world our spiritual determination to live according to the principles of truth, to destroy ignorance and reject falsehood.

On my birthday, on 17 November, all the five hundred Ashram children, devotees of Sri Premananda Ashram, India, and devotees from the Centres around the world came to see me in prison. They broke down its barriers with the force of their pure love and innocence. They covered the walls of the jail with thousands of gloriously coloured flowers and hundreds of lovely garlands. They broke its silence with divine songs in praise of God. Everyone present was sweetened with a chocolate birthday cake made by devotees in the Ashram, which was decorated with the wonderful words of our Ashram symbol: Truth, Purity, Love, Devotion and Wisdom.

With such thoughts of peace and harmony, let us welcome the New Year. You are all welcome to Sri Premananda Ashram at any time. It is a home for helpless children and a spiritual refuge for genuine seekers of the truth. I know who will come to me in 1996. I am waiting for you so that I may bless you with divine treasures.

Many of you have asked me for spiritual guidance especially concerning our tests of 1995. It is essential to understand that everyone who is born as a human being must face a period of trials. Even those who have realized God also have to face such tests if they are born on earth. They often have to bear the jealousy and opposition of those who cannot accept spirituality, genuine innocence, purity and the right, wise path towards the ultimate truth.

Great souls live their lives only to give the message to people that God exists. They have come solely to stress the importance of this, and that humanity should live according to dharma, the eternal, natural code of life. They encourage their devotees and all who come to them to start on the spiritual path in some way, however small.

The power behind the great souls is God's divine force, the shakti. Those people who are full of jealousy and hate oppose the spiritual way and have many selfish desires. Such people do not believe that saints are genuine. They cannot understand or live according to true dharma, and they do not want others to benefit from it either. Because of their own ignorance and lack of spiritual light within, they have always opposed the saints and divine incarnations and given them and their devotees terrible trials and difficulties. Spiritual leaders from all religions have had to face similar situations.

The scriptures and epics of Sanātana Dharma, such as the Mahābhārata and the Rāmāyana, were recorded thousands of years ago. Their stories were relevant to those ancient times, yet their teachings are still of great value even today. However, now times have changed and so God is teaching the masses according to their modern way of life. Yet, whatever the era and whoever the saint undergoing tests for the sake of teaching the people, the truth is one. It is unshakable. You cannot change truth and, finally, it withstands time and all tests. Truth will always win, but you must have patience to realize truth. Like any disease, lies and gossip spread quickly, yet truth always prevails at some stage.

I hold on to truth and continue to guide my devotees to run Sri Premananda Ashram as a pure centre of Divinity, light and love, full of clean hearts and sincere, devoted people. No matter what the obstacles, may truth and purity dispel the darkness of ignorance. May all beings be illumined by the light of the Divine Reality.

I pray for you all and pour out all the love in my heart to you at every moment. I am always here for all of you. Think of those less fortunate than yourselves. Think of those who are hungry, the poor, the many thousands of innocents imprisoned for nothing. We must do something good for them in this lifetime if we can, and not only think of uplifting ourselves.

Pray and think of me. I will always help you. Do not forget this.

With love, light and blessings,

Yours in the Lord, always...

Swami Premananda

# About
# Swami Premananda

From a very young age, Swami Premananda totally devoted his life to spirituality. Prem Kumar Somasundaram was born in 1951 into a merchant family in Matale, Sri Lanka. Whilst still a child he showed signs that he was destined for a spiritual life. As a pet name his parents used to call him Ravi, which means the sun, because of his radiant smile. His special psychic gifts and powers of materialization were evident even as a small child. He demonstrated a passion for religion, spiritual fervour and devotion as well as extraordinary yogic abilities. Ravi's father and mother initially found it difficult to accept their son's fame, which grew as people came to know of his wisdom and extraordinary gifts.

When he was 17, Prem Kumar had a profound inner experience. Swamiji explained, "I wanted to find out what the essence of life was and the purpose of my existence and extraordinary powers (…) I was concentrating so deeply within myself and then...I could see it. I could experience the truth within (…) I established every part of me in the tremendous joy and bliss of the true reality."

After this unalterable experience of the Self, a great peace entered his being. Extraordinary and divine happenings continued and in October 1969 a most unexpected miracle happened. During a spiritual public programme seventeen year old Ravi Swami, wearing his normal white dhoti and shawl, gave a spiritual discourse to around 200 people. Suddenly his clothes miraculously began to change colour into the orange of sannyās (renunciation and monastic life in the Hindu tradition). Ravi Swami was accepted as a sannyāsin only after some time by his family and his name was changed to Swami Premananda. Prema means pure divine love and ānanda means supreme happiness.

Swami Premananda declared that from now on he would totally dedicate himself to spiritual service. He stated that his life's work would be to show the existence and love of God to as many as he possibly could in his lifetime. He started to teach others how to still the mind and experience the truth.

In 1972 he started his first ashram in Matale and more and more people from all walks of life came to experience its peaceful, spiritual environment. He founded a home for needy and homeless children and toured the United Kingdom, Singapore, Malaysia and the Philippines, giving spiritual discourses and programmes.

In 1983 Sri Lanka was rocked by ethnic riots. As he stood for peace and unity, Swami Premananda was a prime target and the beautiful ashram was burnt to the ground. He moved his mission to South India, accompanied by some of the devotees and children from the orphanage and founded a new ashram near Tiruchirappalli. In 1989 the Sri Premananda Ashram was officially inaugurated in the presence of many spiritual leaders. Over the next five years the Ashram flourished. Thousands came every week to listen to Swamiji's brilliant discourses and have a personal interview with him and many destitute children lived and studied in the Ashram. He solved many people's problems and cured their illnesses. A large number of spiritual seekers came from India and abroad, finding their spiritual master and guide towards Self-realization in Swami Premananda.

As his reputation spread there was a bid to blacken his name. In November 1994, in the midst of an extensive defamatory media campaign, in which many false accusations were published, he and six other Ashram residents were arrested and charged with various crimes. Swami Premananda and the others were innocent yet they were convicted and imprisoned despite the fact that witnesses stated they had been forced to speak against him, under duress. Witnesses from around the world testified on his behalf and expert DNA evidence proved that he was innocent.

However, the Ashram activities and those of the Sri Premananda Centres carried on and continue to do so. Despite the entirely false charges, and to the great consternation of his devotees, he was kept in prison for the last 17 years of his life. Yet Swamiji used to smile patiently and say, "I have never committed any crime. I have surrendered totally to divine will. Truth will ultimately win."

As the sandalwood tree transmits its fragrance to whichever tree its roots may touch, Swamiji caused everyone around him to flourish and develop. Swamiji's teachings are universal and enduring. They transcend the barriers of race and religion, inspiring us and bringing us to rest in the Self, beyond the limits of body and mind.

Swamiji left his body on 21st February 2011. His body is interred in a temple in the Ashram in India where miraculous manifestations of vibhūti, sandalwood powder and lingams occur frequently. Swamiji's magnificent presence stays with us and his grace, guidance and teachings continue to uplift and help those who think of him.

# Transliteration and pronunciation of Sanskrit and Tamil

We have used a simple form of transliteration for the convenience of the reader. We have used only the dash on the top of the vowels a, i and u (ā, ī, ū ). This sign shows that the vowel is long as follows:

ā   as in father
ī   as in feed
ū   as in rule

Other vowels are pronounced as follows:
a   as in up or rural
e   as in they
i   as in pin
u   as in full
o   as in more
au  as in how

In Sanskrit there is no th-sound. Therefore the words hatha yoga are pronounced hat-ha yoga. It is the same for all other syllables that contain an h-sound, e.g. b-hajans. The syllable jna in Sanskrit sounds like nya. Words followed by (T) means that they are in the Tamil language.

# Glossary of Sanskrit and Tamil terms

| | |
|---|---|
| **abhishekam** | ritual bathing of a deity while chanting mantras |
| **ādi parāshakti (also called Aum shakti)** | original supreme energy |
| **Agni** | the God of fire, the sacred fire |
| **amrita, amritam (T)** | nectar of immortality |
| **ānanda, ānandam (T)** | highest bliss |
| **āshram, āshrama** | a place of spiritual retreat |
| **asura** | demon |
| **ātma, ātman** | soul, the true Self |
| **ātmikam** | spirituality |
| **Aum, Om** | original cosmic vibration that symbolizes the Divine |
| **Aumkār, Aumkāram** | Aum |
| **avatār** | incarnation of God |
| **bhajan** | devotional song |
| **bhakta** | devotee |
| **bhakti** | devotion |
| **bhūmi** | the earth |
| **brahmacharya** | self-control, celibacy |
| **Brahma muhūrtam (T)** | the time of sunrise considered ideal for spiritual practices |
| **devī** | a goddess, Divine Mother |
| **dharma** | spiritual path, duty |

| | |
|---|---|
| **dhobi (Hindi)** | washerman |
| **dhyāna, dhyānam (T)** | meditation |
| **divya** | divine |
| **divya shakti** | divine force |
| **Durgā** | Hindu goddess in a fierce form |
| **Gangā** | sacred river Ganges in North India that is also respected as a goddess |
| **guru** | one who removes darkness, the spiritual teacher |
| **gurudev** | divine spiritual teacher |
| **guruji** | respected spiritual teacher (adding ji to a name or title is a term of respect) |
| **guru sevā** | service for the guru |
| **hatha yoga** | system of spiritual exercises and methods |
| **ikam** | this world |
| **ishta-devatā** | beloved form of God for worship |
| **ishtam (T)** | beloved form of God for worship |
| **jagat** | the universe, the whole world |
| **jagadjyoti** | universal light |
| **jai prema shānti** | let divine love and peace prevail |
| **japamālā** | string of beads for counting mantras |
| **jīva** | living being, personal soul |
| **jīvātma** | individual soul |

| | |
|---|---|
| **jnāna** | wisdom, knowledge |
| **jnāni** | one who attained supreme knowledge |
| **jyoti** | sacred light |
| **kadavul (T)** | the One who is both within and beyond |
| **karma** | result of past actions |
| **Krishna** | 8th incarnation of Lord Vishnu |
| **kriyā** | yoga of spiritual action |
| **kundalinī** | divine force, at the base of the spine when dormant |
| **Lakshmī** | goddess of spiritual wealth |
| **līlā** | play of the universal energy |
| **lingam** | sacred symbol representing Lord Shiva |
| **Mahābhārata** | Sanskrit epic poem |
| **Mahāshivarātri** | Hindu festival, the great night of Shiva |
| **mahān, mahātma** | great soul |
| **mālā, malar (T)** | garland, necklace, prayer beads |
| **mantra** | sacred formula, words of power, |
| **māyā** | play of illusion |
| **moksha** | liberation |
| **mukti** | release, liberation |
| **mūla** | basis, foundation, causal |
| **mūla mantra** | the original mantra, Om/ Aum |
| **nirvāna** | liberation |

189

| | |
|---|---|
| **Om, Aum** | original cosmic vibration that symbolizes the Divine |
| **Omkār, Omkāram** | Om |
| **paramātma** | Supreme Self, universal soul |
| **paramporul (T)** | original substance |
| **parisuttam (T)** | absolute purity |
| **prema** | divine love |
| **Premānanda** | the bliss of divine love, Swamiji's name |
| **pūjā** | ritual worship |
| **Rāmāyana** | Sanskrit epic poem about the life of Rāma |
| **rishi** | sage, authors of Vedic hymns |
| **sadguru** | authentic spiritual master who is enlightened |
| **sādhana** | regular spiritual practice |
| **sādhu** | saintly person |
| **samādhi** | merging with the Supreme |
| **Sanātana Dharma** | eternal laws and codes of living |
| **sannyās, sannyāsa** | renunciation |
| **sannyāsin** | one who renounces |
| **Sarasvatī** | goddess of knowledge |
| **satsang** | a spiritual discourse or sacred gathering, literally in the company of the highest truth |
| **sattvic** | pure |
| **sevā** | free service, selfless help |
| **sevi jnānam (T)** | wisdom of listening |

| | |
|---|---|
| shakti | divine force |
| shānti | peace |
| shishya | pupil, disciple |
| Shiva | third aspect of the divine Hindu trinity, God of destruction |
| shloka | verse or song of praise |
| siddhi | mystical power |
| summa iru (T) | just be, implying the highest state of conscious being |
| Swami, svāmī | one who is master of himself, a male sannyāsin |
| Vedas | four books that are the basis of the Hindu religion |
| Vedic | pertaining to the Vedas |
| vibhūti | holy ash |
| vīn pechu (T) | useless talk, gossip |
| yāgam | sacrificial fire ceremony |
| yantra | spiritual geometric symbol |
| yoga | union |

Lightning Source UK Ltd.
Milton Keynes UK
UKHW010945160123
415420UK00006B/1213